Sisters said the following actions give them an attitude. . . .

- Men who won't commit but remain marginally in my life, swooping in to get pumped up, sexed up, and fed, then leaving at a moment's notice.
- Being left to take care of the children—their babies—by myself, without support.
- Having to be a "supermom" who does everything for everybody in the whole fucking world.
- Being afraid of being left, over and over and over again by the same damn man, just wearing different pants.
- Getting hit with males' pain and anger, feeling weighted down by their contempt toward me and by their ugly, macho ways.
- Being rejected over and over by men for white, right women, who hardly ever seem to measure up to our (African American women's) beauty.
- Falling in love with every good-looking, two-timing man who comes along.
- Feeling angry about being treated in degrading ways by sexist men who want only parts of me without taking on any responsibility or commitment.
- Feeling so used and spread out that I don't have a moment to exhale—to breathe a little, relax a little, and enjoy the simple pleasures of life.
- Longing for his touch but unable even to get close enough to experience the scent of his body.
- Finding out he's been sleeping around while vowing that he loves me.

Seven Attitude Adjustments for Finding a Loving Man

Audrey B. Chapman

POCKET BOOKS

New York London Toronto Sydney Singapore

An *Original* Publication of POCKET BOOKS

 POCKET BOOKS, a division of Simon & Schuster, Inc.
1230 Avenue of the Americas, New York, NY 10020

ISBN 0-7394-1818-1

POCKET and colophon are registered trademarks of
Simon & Schuster, Inc.

Book design by Christine Weathersbee
Cover design by Jeanne M. Lee; front cover photo by Stone Images

Printed in the U.S.A.

Acknowledgments

Sharing positive feelings about those who have supported and encouraged us is especially appropriate in a book about sharing positive attitudes. I am thankful to many people for their continued belief in the work of enlightening men and women on how healthy love must be shared.

This book could not have been written without the tireless dedication of Elena Oumano, who collaborated in its writing. A special thanks to Judith Andrews, who consulted, encouraged, and influenced with a keen eye the development of the manuscript's focus.

I am grateful to my graphic artist, Ronnie Townes. I would like to give special thanks to my editor, Tracy Sherrod, who recognized the need for this manuscript and believed enough in me that she trusted my ability to deliver on the product. I also give many thanks for her tireless hours of editing.

I would also like to give thanks to my literary agent, Madeleine Morel, who provided tremendous support and encouragement on this project.

Most of all, I am thankful for the stories so many black men and women shared with me so that their situation could be reported. Without them this book could not have been written.

Finally, my heartfelt thanks to all my dear friends and family members for putting up with my absences during this intense period. Without their understanding and adjustment in attitude, I could not have successfully completed this task so others might experience this vital information.

This book is dedicated to all the women that I know and don't know, who have had attitudes, adjusted them, and are now spiritually free thinkers—I love these sisters dearly—Sandra, Cheryl, Julia, Shirley, Leota, Laura, Judith, Elaine, Lois, and Joyce.

I hope the wisdom in this book will shed some light on where we've been and where we don't need to be anymore as women, so that we will always have happiness and love.

If a woman feels like a lady and is able to celebrate herself, she will attract into her life people who reflect her own opinion of herself.

—T. D. JAKES

Contents

The remarkable thing is we have a choice every day regarding the attitude we embrace for that day. We cannot change our past . . . we cannot change the fact that people will act in a certain way. We cannot change the inevitable. The only thing we can do is play on the string we have, and that is our attitude. . . . I am convinced that life is 10 percent what happens to me and 90 percent how I react to it. And so it is with you . . . we are in charge of our attitudes.

—CHARLES SWINDOLL
Attitude: Your Most Important Choice

Introduction

If you are looking for love, but love is nowhere to be found—you are about to embark on a journey within that will point you in the direction of more positive and fulfilling experiences in love and in life.

You will receive all the information and strategies you need to recognize and adjust the defensive attitudes you may have built up over time from struggling with black men. You will take responsibility for past choices and learn how to make healthier ones. You will stop viewing yourself as a victim and begin experiencing yourself as worthy of love and appreciation. You will be able to tell the difference between a brother who is available for the long haul and one who's only there for a hit-and-run. Your energy will be liberated from a prison of negativity, freeing you to create more compassionate situations. You will forget about changing the men in your life because you'll realize that the only person you can change is yourself.

Attitudes don't just happen to black women. They develop after years of repeated romantic disappointments until, finally, a woman becomes overwhelmed with frustration and pain. One fine day, she reaches her limit and begins developing an attitude as a way to cope. She hopes that attitude will disguise her pain from the world and armor her against the threat of any more hurt.

Over and over again, I hear the same blues. The sisters I counsel in my psychotherapy office, who call into my weekly radio show, and pack the audiences at my public speaking engagements all tell me that we are tired of the endless pain, frustration, and disappointment of coping with dysfunctional relationships. We say we are worn-out and fed up with black men's demeaning power games.

Unfortunately, we are too disappointed, disillusioned, angry, and fearful to relax our defenses long enough so we can view the situation with clarity and objectivity. We are so emotionally overwrought that we can't even begin to consider the connection between our romantic troubles and our negative attitudes about relationship choices.

We have become the walking wounded. Traumatized by the war between the sexes, we are locked into a state of mind that could be described as post–traumatic love stress syndrome. Since all that attitude is really an attempt to hide pain, sadness, and loneliness, we rarely smile and our defenses are on hair-trigger alert. We are the head-tossing, eyeball-rolling, hands-on-their-hips sisters who confront the world with, "What the hell are you looking at?" We fail to realize that the attitude we're hiding behind is a total turnoff to men and everyone else alike.

We all know that scientists mix certain chemicals to get a predictable outcome. Attitudes are equally predictable when they mix with certain relationship dynamics. It's a chain reaction. A woman tries to explain to her man what she needs from their relationship, emotionally speaking, and how she feels about the quality of that relationship. Let's say the man doesn't want to hear about it or he is simply not capable of fulfilling her needs. The woman becomes frustrated. Over time, as her emotional needs are consistently unacknowledged, she becomes angry. She also begins doubting herself and her right to expect a man to accept her and give her what she wants. If this pattern is repeated enough times or with enough men, she eventually develops a self-protective attitude as her defense.

A woman named Jan once called in to my radio show so I could help her decide whether to end an eight-month relationship. She told me that she was in love with her boyfriend, but "we have a communication problem."

"What is the problem?" I asked.

She gave me an example: "I wanted him to console me about a difficult legal battle at work. But when I described to him how a supervisor was harassing me, he just said, 'What do you want me to do about it?'"

Jan was hurt, then frightened, because her intuition was telling her that she might have to part ways with this man. After she'd recounted other instances in which her boyfriend either had refused or was unable to be sensitive to her emotional state, it became even more obvious to me that while he wanted to be with her, he didn't want to deal with her problems or needs. I knew that unless Jan accepted that her boyfriend was incapable of being emotionally supportive and that she therefore needed to end the relationship, she would only become even more hurt and frustrated over time. Eventually, she would develop a protective shell and join the ranks of the sisters with attitudes.

What Goes Around Comes Around

In the twenty-five years I've put in as a therapist, struggling to negotiate a truce in this raging, escalating war between black men and women, I've learned that anger only breeds more anger, and hurt breeds more hurt. Yet I have no intention of giving up my hopes of negotiating a treaty. I'm convinced that one glorious day, brothers and sisters will relate in more harmonious ways. Even more crucial, their offspring will finally have the models they so desperately need for healthy adult love based on mutual respect, honesty, support, and most of all, trust.

It saddens me whenever I realize that my progressive, high-achieving clients are so smart about many aspects of their lives, except when it comes to taking care of themselves within a relationship, where they have difficulty negotiating for their needs. When it comes to understanding the reasons they keep landing in painful, degrading situations with the opposite sex and how they can break those negative love patterns, they seem lost and confused. Many of my clients have spent so much time and attention on their careers that they haven't taken enough time to focus on how to find workable solutions that could clear up their love confusion. For some strange reason, most people assume that the emotional experience and maturation any committed relationship requires will automatically fall into place as they grow older. They don't realize that emotional well-being demands the same focused attention, nurturing, and work as getting an education and building a career. Failure to do that work on ourselves is one major reason we're misinformed about love.

You Gotta Pay to Play

Pay to play is an interesting dynamic between today's black men and women all across this country. Both sides are very demanding about what they want from each other, yet both are not willing to give very much of themselves without first being assured of what they're going to get in return. In general, the women want to be treated with respect and as though they're the special, unique one in a man's life. They want promises kept, intentions clear, affection open, and a willingness to share intimacy. And they want the truth, even if it's uncomfortable. On the other hand, men say they want a woman who doesn't give them hassles, who listens, supports, nurtures, and is domestically skilled. In short, a woman should be a safe haven where a man can release the stresses of the day and still feel like "a man."

Each gender talks the talk, but the irony is that neither is willing to walk the walk. No one wants to risk very much at all to get what he or she claims to want. Like a game of chess between two players, someone has to accept the challenge and make a move. Men and women within the black community are stuck in this stalemate, each waiting for the other to go first. So, the relationship becomes an extended game of manipulation, of trying to trick the other person into believing that if they give a little, they will get more. Usually the woman gives in first, then clings to the illusion that she will be rewarded based on the man's vague suggestions that reward is right around the corner.

I remember one afternoon when I was working and I got a telephone call from a friend who was crying hysterically.

"Wait, who is this?" I asked.

"It's me, Candace," I heard through the sobs.

"What's wrong?"

"I'm at Reagan National," she choked out. "I just got in from Ohio, and I was supposed to meet Derek when his plane got in half an hour later. But he's not here! You gotta pick me up now, please!"

I jumped in my car and drove there. I thought she'd be outside, but she was still waiting by the gate where passengers had already disembarked from a plane that had arrived from Denver, Colorado. Candace was just standing there, tears of frustration streaming down her face.

"You just can't count on them!" she began railing as I walked up to her. "I hate all of them! He told me he was moving here from Denver, and I spent all that money traveling back and forth for the past nine months, taking care of him while I was there, using up all my annual leave at work. He promised me he was coming. He told me that he'd changed his local bank account to a national one and that he'd put his résumé on the Internet. He even had me sending him apartment listings from the newspapers here. He was supposed to arrive half an hour ago, but everyone already came off the plane, and he wasn't on it. He didn't even give me the courtesy of a call. I've called him five times on his cell phone, but he won't respond. I've had it with all of them! All I know is the next man is going to pay to play!"

The dynamic between Candace and Derek—she seizing on his insubstantial promises as if they were already reality, then he deciding that he doesn't want to commit after all—plays out over and over again between countless black men and women. How did we get to this place where it seems as if only master players can survive the game of love? Where both sides are more concerned about winning and being the one in control than in enjoying a stable relationship in which each tries to meet the other's needs? Few people these days seem willing to risk what all deep relationships require—allowing oneself to be emotionally vulnerable. If only black couples could understand that yielding to each other's emotional state of mind can be less unstable, more caring, and loving.

Black men and women these days are heavily invested in not becoming vulnerable to each other because they equate vulnerability with weakness. They don't want to risk that loss of power. In their minds, if one partner wins, that must mean the other is the loser. They don't believe that both partners can win at love. Yet to develop love between two people, both partners must be willing to risk surrendering so that both parties might be empowered together. Once they have the confidence to accept this fact, they will be assured that whatever happens, their relationship will survive.

This information is not only important for individual men and women but for the entire black community. Once we are able to grasp the importance of allowing ourselves to be compassionate to each other, our relationships will improve. And improving relationships between individual men and women has to be the root of any positive changes within the black family and the black community at large.

Fixing What's Broken

Male-female relationships have suffered terribly from the many cultural shifts that have taken place over the past few decades. At best, men now feel ambivalent toward women, and women experience a great deal of pain and bitterness. Many of today's single men and women are lonely. They attempt to ease the loneliness with a frenzy of social activity, but that satisfaction never lasts. Over the long run, they're left with feelings of emptiness and discouragement. Sadly, black romantic partnerships in America are undergoing the greatest struggle to pull it together.

The prospects may appear bleak, but I have written this book because I refuse to believe that black men and women have given up on each other altogether.

Many of us, regardless of race, are searching for love. The problem is that too few of us are willing to pay the price of commitment—doing the necessary work and making the necessary sacrifices. That's because not many of us know what love really is. We think it's a *feeling*, but in fact, it's an *action* derived straight from the heart and soul.

I wrote those lines immediately after viewing on television the Million Family March that took place on October 16,

2000. Just a couple of generations ago, we wouldn't have needed a march to affirm the importance of a loving relationship between a man and a woman and taking responsibility for our families. It was clear to my parents and grandparents that forming a strong family unit was the most effective way to survive living in America.

Black folks in America have been caught up in one of the major social shifts that took place back in the seventies when women demanded equal rights and the focus switched from looking out for the collective need to satisfying each individual's desires. The confusion we're experiencing right now is a direct outcome of that "me movement" that places less value on unions than on "doing your own thing."

Black men and women are also reacting as a whole to negative models of oppression and abuse that they witnessed between their parents, even though those parents placed a stronger commitment on keeping family together. This has created a backlash: many younger people can't see the benefits of committing to partnerships. Women don't want to be like their mothers, who worked unfulfilling jobs and came home to a demanding husband and children or were left alone by men to support and raise their children. Many men don't see the point of marriage or commitment. During their parents' day, their fathers were emotionally distant, not on the scene at all, or hardly ever at home, because they were so burdened by economic pressures that they worked as many as three jobs.

Today's men and women regard each other as items in a long list of disposable goods. In fact, the hassles of commitment make love something to avoid, instead of an ideal to attain. Some men and women have concluded that relationships are too much trouble; while others have decided to relate to each other on the basis of "let's make a deal: I'll give you 'this,' if you do 'that.' " For instance, a woman might want company and an escort for various functions from time to time, while the man might want limited closeness and occasional sexual intimacy. So, they strike a deal.

We simply will not risk the pitfalls of love to gain its benefits. Unlike older generations, who understood that love does not come without conditions and compromises, the new black man and woman want active social lives with high-quality bedmates, without the price tag of commitment. Yet commitment is essential for true emotional fulfillment and mature love. Avoiding commitment means that you are cheating yourself of the greatest benefit of being in a relationship: it forces you to confront your issues and take ownership of them. This aspect of relationships may seem troublesome and can certainly stir up attitudes.

Many black people fight this notion that being in a relationship means they have to become somewhat introspective and take the time to understand and work on their issues. But the black family and the community as a whole will never be secure until individuals take responsibility for their own stuff. It's not about dressing up and looking good. It's about going inside yourself and cleaning up what's not so pretty. This is a courageous act that takes lots of effort and devotion. Making these sacrifices and hanging in there takes great devotion, but unless enough of us work on ourselves, future generations will be in even worse trouble than we are today.

PART I

ATTITUDE

The capacity to love is so tied to being able to be awake, to being able to move out of yourself and be with someone else in a manner that is not about your desire to possess them, but to be with them, to be in union and communion.

—BELL HOOKS,
Salvation: Black People and Love

One

What Makes Sisters Want to Shout?

One Saturday afternoon a month, I attend my women's book club. It never ceases to amaze me that no matter what we're reading, whether it's a novel or a self-help book, the conversation always drifts to the men in our lives.

One afternoon, we'd just finished talking about Yolanda Joe's *He Say, She Say,* a novel about black relationships that switches back and forth between the male and female characters' points of view. Reading about how differently the men and women viewed their relationships naturally got everyone thinking about their own situations.

"Gloria, that father really reminded me of your doggish boyfriend," said Lenore. "You know, the way he runs the streets and doesn't show up when he's supposed to half the time."

"Why are you being so hard on the brother?" retorted Gloria. "The man's just going through something!"

Sheena jumped right in: "They're always going through

something! I'm sick of them! And I'm sick of sisters making excuses for their tired behavior."

"Nobody ever makes excuses for us sisters," Betti agreed. "And I think that's unfair."

"Who ever told you that life would be fair in the first place?" Hazel retorted.

"I've had some fairness in my life from some brothers," said Cassandra. "Problem is, just as I was starting to relax and enjoy it, they would always do something stupid."

"Like what, for instance?" asked Gloria.

"Like tell me that he'd just started working for some pyramid sales company and he'd be hanging out at the meetings, recruiting until about two in the morning," Cassandra explained.

Everyone roared with laughter.

"Girl, don't go for that," said Enid. "That's a highly unlikely story. Sounds to me like brotherman is just handing you a big, big lie."

"But I remember when one of our ex–club members, Jackie, was coming every month, complaining about being stood up," said Tess. "None of you ever pointed out to her that her misery was really because she chose to see a married man. No one except me ever told her that she was responsible for her own misery because she was dealing with a man who she knew was already committed."

"Why do you girls always have to talk about these men?" said Barbara. "We all know that they're hopeless. They're only good for three things: sex, carrying heavy loads, and good times. When are you all going to get smart and start taking care of yours?"

"All right, girls, I think we've gone beyond what we're here for," I cut in. "We're getting into deep water, and if we don't get back to this book, we're all going to leave here today with attitudes."

When black women share with me the stories of their frustrating love lives, they usually believe that they're telling me something new. Unfortunately, I hear similar tales of woe from virtually every new client. Over the years, I've observed that the defensive behaviors we adopt in order to live with our pain shape themselves around seven "attitudes."

Attitude One—Rage:

"Don't even try to mess with me." "I'm angry and everybody's gonna get it!" The need to let off anger and sarcasm on any available target.

Attitude Two—Control:

"Man, where were you last night?" The drive to control one's environment and the people in it.

Attitude Three:—Desperation:

"I'm gonna make you love me." The overwhelming need to be rescued and loved, at any cost.

Attitude Four—Materialism:

"Ain't nothing going on but the rent." Filling an emotional void with the pursuit of platinum, BMWs, and Versace.

Attitude Five—Mothering:

"Come to Momma, baby." The drive to nurture that masks a hidden demand to be nurtured oneself.

Attitude Six—Shame:

"Without a man, I'm nothing." The humiliation of being single, alone in a world where everyone else seems to come in couples.

Attitude Seven—Cynicism:

"All men are sorry." "Men ain't nothing but trouble." The insistence that all brothers are dogs and unfit for a loving, trusting, monogamous relationship.

I will explore each of these attitudes in greater detail in chapter 3.

These seven "deadly" attitudes get women through the night, so to speak, but they do not really ease the pain, and they certainly don't correct the fundamental problem. Keep in mind that whatever you put out into the world, you are certain to get back.

Once you are willing to confront the behaviors and attitudes that get you in trouble—often without your even knowing it—you won't need to be angry and you will no longer suffer that terrible pain. If your thinking is bound up in attitudes of fear, resentment, or cynicism, it is difficult to take a good, long, hard look at yourself. You're too busy blaming everyone else for your own mess. If you continue refusing to look within so you can examine how your own issues and decisions may be getting you into trouble, you won't change your beliefs or your patterns of behavior. In other words, you won't adjust your attitude so that when the right man does come along, you recognize him and choose to share with him a positive, loving relationship.

You may be shaking your head right now, wondering, what's the point? Is there any hope, any way out between the rock of black women's bad attitudes and the hard place of black men's bad behaviors? "Why bother to adjust my attitude?" you could be asking yourself. "A man won't change by wanting to love me anyway. What's the payoff?"

Let me assure you that the payoff for adjusting your attitude is well worth the trouble of taking a good, hard look within. Here are three good reasons you should make that adjustment:

- **Personal self-understanding.** One, if you are overwhelmed by bitterness and hostility, it doesn't matter how attractive you are, how educated, how religious, how beautifully dressed, how much money you have, or how exquisite your home. None of those externals will get you what you want—even if one hundred Mr. Rights were to turn up on your doorstep—if all those blessings are tainted by a sour, angry, desperate, or fearful attitude. Men are equipped with built-in radar for a bad attitude, and they will take any action to avoid it. More important, attitude is everything in life. It influences all aspects of your experience and plays a huge role in your choices and what happens to you. It's pretty miserable lugging around a crusty, hard attitude that colors every aspect of your day. That bad day becomes a week,

then a month, a year, a decade, until, finally, your attitude has cast a pall over your entire life.

- **Living a happy life.** Two, maintaining a negative attitude saps a lot of the energy you could be using to be
  more creative, productive, and even have more fun in
  your life.
- **Personal growth.** Three, hanging on to a self-protective
  but self-defeating attitude suggests that just because you
  can't find the man you want, life is over, a done deal.

"It's Saturday Night and I Ain't Got Nobody"

As the host of *The Audrey Chapman Show*—a weekly Saturday-
morning radio program broadcast in Delaware; Washington,
D.C.; Virginia; and Maryland—I tackle virtually all the issues
that come up between black women and men. About two years
ago, we aired a show entitled "It's Saturday Night and I Ain't
Got Nobody," after Wilson Pickett's classic tune. We didn't
think much about it, except in terms of people being home
alone on Saturday night, but as soon as we announced the
morning's topic, the switchboard was flooded with calls. Most
of my callers are usually women, but this time, the brothers
were burning up the wires, eager to express shock and dismay
that so many ladies were home alone on Saturday night. In
fact, we received so many calls that we had to repeat the show
the following week.

The women who called my show about Saturday-night
dates expressed hurt, sadness, confusion, and anger, because

they didn't have a clue about how to fill their long, empty, solitary weekends. Some of those women had dropped out of the social scene because they'd never been able to get past their confusion. They gave up because they couldn't grasp why they had kept on selecting certain types of men who never worked out for them, and they'd never taken time to consider what kind of man would actually have suited them better.

I wondered how many women actually had a clear idea of what kind of man they wanted to be with on Saturday or any other night of the week. Have you taken time to think about what traits you really want in a man? Good listener, honest, reliable, etc. Sometimes, a good place to begin getting clear about what you want in a man is to make a list of ten or more traits you know you definitely *do not* want. List those traits here:

Traits I Don't Want in a Man

1.

2.

3.

4.

5.

6.

7.

8.

9.

10.

Now, you are ready to make up a list of ten or more traits you do want in a man:

Traits I Do Want in a Man

1.

2.

3.

4.

5.

6.

7.

8.

9.

10.

If your lists are too long for these pages, write them on a separate sheet of paper. Make sure to keep them handy. After you finish reading this book, check your lists again to see if you want to make any changes. Notice those changes. These lists will help provide you with a new awareness so that you can distinguish between what you *think* you want in a man and what traits are really best for you.

Making these lists will also help you to become more selective during the dating process. Immediately, you will recognize a man who seems to have the qualities that you desire.

It seems that more sisters than ever are singing the lonely-lady blues. Studies confirm that the numbers of unmarried black adults—males and females—is at an all-time high. A 1999 report put out by the Morehouse Research Institute, *Turning the Corner on Father Absence in Black America,* found that 70 percent of black children are now born to single black mothers. Linked to that dismal statistic is a divorce rate that is currently nearly twice as high in the black community as the white. According to Professor Larry Davis of the Research Institute, two out of every three black marriages end in divorce, compared to one in every two white marriages. In 1970, the U.S. Census Bureau found one unmarried couple living together for every one hundred households with married couples. Today, the Census Bureau reports that the figure has soared to eight unmarried partners for every one hundred who are married. Based on surveys conducted in 1997, the bureau states that "nearly 35 percent of Americans aged twenty-five to thirty-four have never been married. Among African-Americans, the figure is 54 percent." Other studies find that black women who divorce are unlikely to marry again.

So, Daddy's not at home. He's having children without getting married, or he's getting divorced twice as frequently as three decades ago, and the pool of single black women who will never marry is larger than ever before in American history. In other words, we now have the perfect situation to ignite widespread panic and desperation in black women of all ages. Even if a sister married at twenty years old or so and later divorced, by the time she hits her midforties, she's been "out there" for about two decades. By then, the pickings look mighty slim. Many men are in committed relationships, and some men are gay and don't relate to women romantically. Others relate only to women of other ethnic and racial groups.

Yet another group has an addiction problem or is incarcerated, under- or unemployed, or has deep-seated issues about women that make them poor candidates for permanency.

All this sparks a second rush of desperation. "I'm getting older," a woman thinks. "Now there's even less to choose from!" No wonder so many black women are weighted down by a deep sense of hopelessness, frustration, and depression that's so often masked by the outward facade of an angry attitude. More often the anger is a protective defense to cover up sadness and deep longing.

Black women feel cheated. They want to build and sustain romantic relationships with black men, yet it looks to them as if the relatively few brothers who are "marriage material" resist this prospect in every way that they can. Some black women even believe that black men just don't like them. At the very least, they sense that many black men don't want to relate to them in a serious way and that brothers have virtually opted out of marriage and commitment.

The Sisters' Blues Ain't Like Everyone Else's

According to the American Psychological Association (APA), women are more susceptible to depression than men because they are less likely to feel in control of their lives and more likely to dwell on their problems. Unfortunately, more sisters are depressed than in other groups of women.

The National Mental Health Association states that almost 50 percent more black women experience depression than do women of other races. Studies also find that black women are more often subject to the many stress factors that lead to depression: poverty, sexual or physical abuse, discrimination, loss of employment, crime, violence, and the death of a loved one. Those findings are backed up by the March 6, 1999, issue of *Advance Data,* a publication put out by the U.S. Centers for Disease Control and Prevention (CDC).

In his *Washington Post* column published January 19, 1999, titled "The Happiness Study," African-American writer Courtland Milloy cites the CDC's conclusion that black women experience "bad feelings" at a rate three times as high as white men. In fact, according to the CDC, black women are the least happy people in America.

Milloy writes that he was so shocked by these conclusions that he took to the streets to conduct his own informal survey to match his own data to the CDC's findings. After presenting the scientific findings to random sisters and receiving universal "So, what else is new?" reactions, one woman finally laid it out for Milloy: "Of course we are the most unhappy. We are women *and* we are black." Another woman worked with a team of black men at BET TV. She stated that the male workers there often dragged their heels, forcing the women to shoulder most of the workload. This made those sisters not only unhappy in love but also miserable throughout each day of the work week.

"Could it be that black women actually are being treated worse than any other group?" Milloy speculates. He then paraphrases an anonymous black sociologist who "theorized that part of the problem may be that African-American women, as some of the most liberated and independent women on earth, unfortunately have been mismatched with some of the most sexist, insecure, and self-excusing of men."

That anonymous male sociologist's theory is supported by results from another poll of black women on the state of their love relationships that was conducted in 1993 by *The Atlanta Journal-Constitution*. Of the Southern black women who participated, 68 percent stated that their relationships with black men had changed over the years for the worse.

What Makes Sisters Want to Shout?

At least some of the stress factors that make sisters prone to depression and to acting out their pain and frustration through attitudes involve their difficult relationships with men. I conducted my own survey into exactly what types of male behavior trouble black women most. During a public speaking appearance, I asked the women in my audience to answer in writing, "What makes sisters want to shout?" Here are some of their answers:

- Men who won't commit but remain marginally in your life, swooping in to get pumped up, sexed up, and fed, then leaving you at a moment's notice.
- Being left to take care of the children—their babies—by yourself, without support.
- Having to be a "supermom" who does everything for everybody in the whole fucking world.
- Being afraid of being left, over and over and over again by the same damn man, just wearing different pants.

- Getting hit with their pain and anger, feeling weighted down by their contempt toward you and by their ugly, macho ways.
- Being rejected over and over by men for white, right women who hardly ever seem to measure up to our beauty.
- Falling in love with every good-looking, two-timing man who comes along.
- Feeling angry about being treated in degrading ways by sexist men who want only parts of you without taking on any responsibility or commitment.
- Feeling so used and spread out that you don't have a moment to exhale—to breathe a little, relax a little, and enjoy the simple pleasures of life.
- Longing for his touch but unable even to get close enough to experience the scent of his body.
- Finding out that he's been sleeping around while vowing that he loves you.

These remarks make it clear that sisters are frustrated by the treatment they receive from men. And, too often, we feel that venting our pain through insults is our only salvation.

Battling between Brothers and Sisters

I received another graphic picture of the anger and pain created by the war between brothers and sisters when I delivered a talk on male-female relationships during Black History Month at Virginia's historically black Hampton University.

The audience consisted of five hundred students and faculty.

I shared with my audience the results of an informal survey conducted by Indianapolis University concerning levels of trust between men and women. The survey question: When was the last time you shared a truly intimate secret with someone of the opposite sex? Only ten percent said they had ever shared an intimate secret with a partner. What did my audience think the level of trust was between Hampton's men and women? I asked.

A huge roar of laughter welled up, especially from the young men, who seemed particularly tickled by the word *trust* mentioned in the same breath as *women*. "What's this all about?" I wondered aloud. One young woman approached a microphone set up in the audience.

"You can't trust them," she said decisively. "They're all over the place with everybody on this campus."

"It's not just that *we're* all over," a young man countered. "Y'all make it easy!"

Those words kicked off a hot debate. Another woman jumped up to get at a microphone.

"You guys just need to grow up!" she declared.

"In what areas do they need to grow up?" I asked.

"They need to learn how to be more honest," she explained. "Why is it that whenever you question a guy about his intentions, you can't get an honest answer?"

The bickering between the Hampton women and men reflects the raging war between black women and men of all ages. We're making a big mistake if we believe the war is only between youngsters or includes merely a few individuals. In fact, we need to examine the ongoing "battling" within the context of what's going on in America overall.

Since the seventies, this country has moved steadily in the direction of disposability, superficiality, and the impersonal, "free" sex mentality that was jump-started by birth control pills, Masters and Johnson's sexuality studies, and the founding of *Playboy* and *Cosmopolitan* magazines. Whether married or unmarried, people were urged during that era to "do your own thing." A mild backlash followed the initial explosion of sexual freedom so that people were still openly sexual, but unwed mothers and unmarried cohabitation were frowned upon. Abortion became legal but remained somewhat undercover.

In the mideighties, herpes and HIV infection raised their ugly heads, so the public discourse switched to safe sex. What went missing from both eras—the excitement of sexual freedom in the seventies and the warnings about safe sex from the eighties up to the present—has been any talk about how to develop the insights and skills that allow people to form lasting, loving attachments. Some people today are struggling to figure out how to create families, while other families continue to fall apart as divorce becomes a more common solution to relationship problems. In addition, increasing numbers of women are choosing career over marriage.

The gap between sexual engagement and emotional commitment that first appeared in the seventies has grown into a yawning chasm. People are more disillusioned than ever over the widening separation between sex and emotional connection. In the black community especially, it seems as if men and women have never been more at odds.

An article in the February 18, 2000, issue of *Hilltop,* Howard University's weekly student paper, discusses a controversial interview with actor Wesley Snipes that appeared in a 1996 edition of *Ebony* magazine. Snipes admitted in that interview to his preference for submissive Asian women who would "give me peace in my home." Here is what the Howard student writer thinks of Snipes's choice:

> Snipes' decision to eschew Black women, in favor of Asians, was based upon a long-standing trial-and-error basis—not a knee-jerk "dark gentlemen prefer blondes motif." Snipes' decision, and every other Black man that [*sic*] finds love outside of boa-constrictor-like Social Hermaphrodism of Black women, deserves to be honored and respected without any mouth from the Sapphire Gestapo. Our freedom of choice is evidence of our humanity, and any white, black or female [*sic*] that [*sic*] tries to deny us our birthright as men is practicing a nuanced racism no less deadly than the Ku Klux Klan or the Nazi party.
>
> Wesley Snipes was speaking for all Black men. What the Black man wants is respect, submission, cooperation, peace, companionship, and regular sex with a conviction to please. . . . Slavery and our tragic history has [*sic*] spoiled the Black female, and she is misguided to believe that her closed-shop vaginal-monopoly over her Black brother is permanent.

Sadly, this young black male writer's list of what brothers want from sisters does not even mention "love," and the sexist, macho, and emotionally detached persona he displays in his writing is shared by too many of his peers.

In *More Than Sex: Reinventing the Black Male Image,* George Edmond Smith, M.D., exposes the roots of that macho, sexist, and emotionally detached persona in a deep and pervasive insecurity:

> The enigma that the African-American male must solve is why must he define himself through his sexuality? Must the black man confirm his manliness by how many beautiful women he has had? More importantly, why is another person's perception so important to the black man's image? There's a deep-rooted insecurity in African-American men as the result of sexual stereotyping. If all black men have to offer is the ability to satisfy a woman, then doesn't it stand to reason that we would have to keep satisfying women sexually to prove that we have something to offer? As a result, emotions become difficult to express and men become terrified of the possibilities of rejection.

As every adult should know, sex alone can't sustain a relationship and make it last. The refusal of many black men to offer more than sex is one of the key reasons for the war between black men and women.

The Numbers Game

My friend Lorraine and I were talking one day about her divorce and all our girlfriends' discouraging romantic experiences.

"I don't know when we're finally going to realize that there's only four," Lorraine said.

"Four what?" I asked.

"Four men in the entire world who understand what relationships are all about. You gotta be lucky enough to be in the right place at the right time to meet one of the four. If you don't, you just spend all your life in search of, encountering, and being grossly disappointed."

"How discouraging this would be for so many women if they were to buy into what you're saying," I objected. "It makes the situation nearly hopeless!"

"Not if they're willing to struggle with a man. Quite frankly, I've given up the struggle. I'm just gonna love 'em and leave 'em."

Sadly, many black women agree that their sole choices are to be alone or to stay in a relationship that shortchanges their needs. Lorraine has decided that she prefers to be alone. That numbers game is distracting her—and perhaps you—from the reality that good men are out there, and there're more than four!

Are You a Sister with Attitude?

Is your love style getting you into emotional trouble, causing you to develop negative attitudes and to engage in behavior that sabotages your chances for a genuine love partnership?

If you want to explore this possibility and identify the thoughts and belief systems that are keeping you stuck, you first need to pinpoint your personal love style. The following questions will help you discover what behaviors may be fueling your cycle of anger, pain, shame, and fear. Check *yes, no,* or *sometimes* after each question:

1. Do you move quickly into dating situations by planning out the next several months of social events with each new man?
Yes_____ No_____ Sometimes_____

2. Do you make excuses for a man's bad behavior and ignore the clues telling you he's emotionally or socially unavailable?
Yes_____ No_____ Sometimes_____

3. Do you fantasize about receiving constant attention, material indulgences, and fulfillment of other needs by a particular man (or any man)?
Yes_____ No_____ Sometimes_____

4. Do you believe that because of the male shortage, you have to accept any type of treatment from a man, no matter how degrading or insensitive, just to avoid rejection and loss?
Yes_____ No_____ Sometimes_____

5. Do you find yourself attracted only to men who need financial and/or emotional help, especially yours?
Yes_____ No_____ Sometimes_____

6. Do you have sex right off the bat, then assume that your time in bed means the man is seriously committed?
Yes_____ No_____ Sometimes_____

7. Do you often find yourself getting into arguments or feeling irritated and upset over minor events and inconveniences?

   Yes_____ No_____ Sometimes_____

8. Do you refuse to attend public events by yourself, from parties to the neighborhood movie theater, because you're afraid people will think you're a loser?

   Yes_____ No_____ Sometimes_____

9. Do you renege on social commitments as soon as you meet a man, even if it means breaking a date with a female friend at the last moment?

   Yes_____ No_____ Sometimes_____

10. Do you believe that if you do everything to please a man, he will "learn to love you"?

    Yes_____ No_____ Sometimes_____

11. Do you believe that men can only offer you sex, good times, and money?

    Yes_____ No_____ Sometimes_____

12. Do you believe that because all men are cheaters, they shouldn't be taken seriously?

    Yes_____ No_____ Sometimes_____

If you answered *yes* or *sometimes* to just one question, you need this book. You may believe that your attitude doesn't need adjusting, but I invite you to read on, anyway. Our minds play games on us now and then in order to lead us away from the discomfort that often comes up whenever we confront our own truths.

Perhaps you had difficulty answering the questions clearly and honestly. In that case, skip them for now. After you've read a few more chapters, return to these pages and attempt to answer the questions again. You will find that you are better able to identify your personal love style and behavior patterns. You will begin to see ways in which you can stop these automatic ways of reacting to men and others around you.

Try to remain open. Every one of us could use a little enlightenment from time to time. These questions are a first step toward greater awareness of how what you are putting out is determining what you're getting back.

In the next several chapters, you'll learn much more about how your own defensive attitudes and misguided behaviors create your unhappiness, and you will discover ways to replace them with a more positive, empowered attitude. You will no longer see yourself as a victim. You will realize that you are capable of clear, positive choices, and you will know that you are worthy of love and appreciation. The strategies and insights you gain will divert all that energy you've been wasting on negative situations toward creating better situations that enhance your life. Most important, your focus will shift from changing the men in your life to changing yourself.

This "me first" is critical. Until you change your own approach to life and love, it won't matter what man you meet along the way. Until you put a *constructive* "me first" into place, you will continue to let life happen to you instead of learning how to think strategically and directing the course of your life.

That conscious "me first" will help you tap into your personal power. Later on in the book we will deal more fully with personal power and its relationship to self-awareness. You will see that once you possess the self-awareness you need in order to form positive, lasting relationships, you will become more secure and less defensive. You will take care of yourself with men, without ever becoming hostile or bitter.

I'm not guaranteeing that you will meet Mr. Right and spend the rest of your days hand in hand, walking into the sunset together. I do guarantee, though, that after you remove the blinders of your attitudes, you will see the way to lasting love far more clearly. At the very least, you will move from desperation, anger, hostility, cynicism, or shame about being alone to a more hopeful position of self-acceptance and inner peace. You will be released from your pain and open to a more self-fulfilling life.

You need to make
the changes within
yourself that you
seek in others.

Two

Different Men, Same Problems

Tina was tired and frustrated. Forty was approaching fast, and she was still alone. Except for a brief marriage to a college sweetheart that had ended when he'd left her for another woman, Tina had been single most of her adult life.

"Men are no good," she spat out as she sat across from me in my office. "You can't trust them; they're always looking for a better deal."

Tina's temper flared up when I asked questions that changed the focus from men to her: "What are you really looking for in a relationship?" "Why do you think things always go badly for you?" "What role do you think you play in your own unhappiness?"

"You make it sound like it's all my fault," she argued. "You know how black men are."

Tina's attitudes about men and her defensive reaction to my suggestion that her own thinking and behavior played a negative role in her love life are typical of many single black women. They are tired of being alone. They desperately want a romantic partner, but they fear that their options are limited. Even black women who are in relationships constantly worry about competition from all the single black women they know.

With or without a man, black women always seem to come up losers. They either waste their time fretting about the men they can't find or worrying about how to keep the one they do have faithful. That fear of ultimate loss is the reason many black women are stuck and terribly unhappy.

After years of rejection or mistreatment by men, many black women begin to define their sense of self on the basis of whether they are accepted or rejected. If they've been rejected too many times, their self-esteem suffers terribly.

If your self-image depends upon the acceptance of others, you are riddled with self-doubt. Any rejection will plunge you into sadness, anger, bitterness, and fear. To defend yourself from the pain of those feelings, you learn to protect yourself with the disguise of a bad attitude. You wrap yourself in the hardened veneer of that bad attitude to present the world with a false image that you are on top of the situation and also to create the ultimate shield from any more hurt and disappointment.

Yet these attitudes and the negative behaviors associated with them eventually overwhelm your life, negating your chance for a romantic relationship or any happiness in life at all!

In a passage from Terry McMillan's *How Stella Got Her Groove Back,* Stella is trying to decide whether she'll return to Jamaica for a rendezvous with the young man she'd met there. As she pours out her suspicions and fears to a friend, Stella neatly describes the sisters' dilemma:

"I'm wondering why this young man really wants to sleep with me. What is the attraction? What is the real motive? I know. He's probably heard the rumor going around America that single women over thirty and black women in particular will fuck anything, since many of them are on that slow track. They used to count how many weeks had gone by since they'd been laid but now it's gotten up to how many years has it been and they're all freaking out because they're super lonely and in their quest to find Mr. Perfect for years and years have yet to come to the realization that he does not exist. We who have labeled ourselves Ms. Fucking Perfect Personified have not caught on yet that our perfection is merely a figment of our very own distorted imagination and I should know because I'm in that forty and over club for Emotional Subversive in Denial About Everything."

Stella and many women like her "guard their hearts" with self-protective attitudes. However, their need to connect with a man remains just as strong and urgent. With each failed romantic encounter, their frustration and heartbreak increase, until that pain takes over their lives and leads them to make even more impetuous and poorly thought-out choices that trap them deeper in their swamp of unhappiness and confusion. So much bitterness, fear, and anger build up that the woman presents herself to the world with the hands-on-her-hips-approach-me-if-you-dare persona that, unfortunately, stereotypes all black women.

Where is the payoff for all the years of sacrifice, women

want to know. Black women are convinced that they are the "backbone" of the black community, the ones who struggle to hold everything together, and the ungrateful black man has let them down. The women want what the majority of all women want—a man to love and care for them. Yet, they contribute to their own dilemma by blaming men and failing to consider how their own behavior and attitudes may be contributing to their unhappiness.

Whether they're in their early teens, their twenties, thirties, forties, or beyond, I see too many black women struggling for love without getting anywhere near it. It's as if they're caught in what I call a Wheel of Misfortune.

The illustration on page 30 shows how you can become trapped in that Wheel of Misfortune. It also points out the way to get out of that trap.

Keeping the Faith

I first realized that the majority of black women are stuck in this wheel of disappointment, frustration, and hopelessness when I was on a promotional tour for my last book, *Getting Good Loving: How Black Men and Women Can Make Love Work*. Some sisters wanted to know why they needed a self-help book about love when there was no love in sight. I particularly remember one woman in her forties. "Why on earth did you write a book about love and black men when the two don't even go together?" she wanted to know. Then she walked off without even waiting for my answer, muttering to herself, "I've given up on black men."

WHEEL OF MISFORTUNE

THE WAY OUT
ACCEPTANCE OF OPTIONS
TRUSTING
BONDING/INTIMACY
LOVE
COMMITMENT

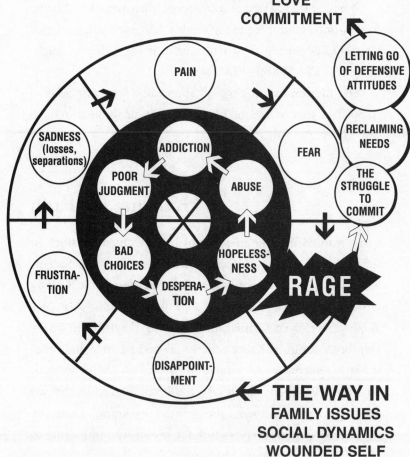

THE WAY IN
FAMILY ISSUES
SOCIAL DYNAMICS
WOUNDED SELF

That woman personified an attitude shared by many black women who tell me that they've lost faith in the possibility that any black man will ever make a loving, lasting commitment to them.

Some black women who've lost faith choose to endure punishing relationships. They're afraid to be alone, and they're convinced that they can't do any better. Others have come to view any conflict in romance as just another hassle that they don't need. They tell me they want romantic relationships to serve as an escape from a harsh, unfair, and troublesome world. As a result, they are unable to tolerate even the least bit of conflict or frustration within a relationship and the discomfort of trying to work it out. They are virtual time bombs, ready to explode at the slightest disappointment. Their unrealistic expectations disconnect them completely from the possibility of finding a good man and establishing a lasting commitment.

Black women who earn fairly decent salaries, live in their own homes, and drive their own cars decide after numerous romantic disappointments that "I can do bad by myself." That attitude dovetails neatly with the feelings of some black men: "Since you don't seem like you need us, since you got it so together, we'd rather be with women who focus on our needs." Adding to that unfortunate combination of attitudes is the catch-22 dilemma faced by the black woman who spent her younger years pursuing an education and career instead of a man. When she's finally ready for a commitment, she learns, much to her dismay, that the older the woman, the fewer the men left in the pool, especially the black male pool. Plus, those available men who are lower down on the economic totem pole are often so threatened by an accomplished woman that they become competitive instead of supportive.

Love's Dead Ends: Pretty Boys, Bad Boys, and Star Boys

Many black women who've given up on finding Mr. Right settle instead for a series of superficially attractive Mr. Wrongs. Some of these sisters thrive on flashing trophy men before the "competition," as if these men were expensive trinkets. Trophy men include pretty boys, bad boys, star-jock boys, and any other man a woman wants for superficial reasons.

Many women attribute their desire to be with trophy men to a yen for the excitement of hooking up with a major player or the thrill of cuddling up to danger. They rarely admit to any other motives. Yet a key motive for going after trophies is to beat out the competition. Sisters are fiercely competitive over men. Landing any man is a major coup these days, and if he's also pretty, bad, or star material, then you become, by association, the fiercest sister of your social set. You're the envy of every other woman who sees you with him, particularly your friends. You get to hear them say, "Girlfriends, did you see the fine man she was with last night!"

Again, women who pursue trophies claim that they just wanna have fun and that these boys are more exciting than the nice guys. Trophies are in control of the game and they know it, so they make for a good challenge to a woman's seductive powers. A woman named Eva once told me that she is immediately attracted to a good-looking, shady type of guy who comes across in an arrogant, cocky way. It's easier for her to be with a man like him, she confided, because he puts it all out there and she knows what he's all about.

Another reason women chase pretty boys, bad boys, and star-jock boys is to share the extravagant lifestyle they believe many white women enjoy as a birthright. Still other sisters go for these men because they feel their own lives are unexciting and dull. They don't feel sure of themselves overall because they haven't worked on developing their minds or their social skills. As a result, these women place way too much value on how a man looks or on his status, because they expect his borrowed starlight will brighten their own world.

Sadly, trophy hunters often have "nice" guys in their lives, but they don't want nice guys. In fact, a male friend once told me that being dubbed a nice guy is a man's idea of the kiss of death.

After one woman I know survived a grueling ordeal with a superstar pretty boy, she realized with hindsight that the main reason she'd pursued him so desperately and put up with his shoddy treatment was because "he made me look good within my social circle of friends."

Needless to say, if you really want Mr. Right, don't go looking for him amongst those romantic dead ends. All you'll end up with is disappointment, a sagging ego, and a bad attitude.

Bad Attitudes

Black women are not only more depressed than everyone else, they're angrier. Harvard professor Orlando Patterson's research concludes that African-American women experience anger more often and for longer periods than any other group, male or female.

In *Rituals of Blood: Consequences of Slavery in Two American Centuries*, Patterson states that "nearly 40 percent of African-American women feel angry either continuously or for several days, compared with a third of Euro-American women and 24 percent of men of both ethnic groups."

Patterson's most troubling discovery in his research on black women's anger was that, more often than not, black women refuse to accept the source of their anger. The source of that anger, Patterson makes clear, is black men.

Yes, black women will complain about their men 24–7, but they've also been defending and protecting black men throughout American history as a throw down from slavery. Some ladies stay detached from what they feel so they can play the game of denial and continue to deal with the brother and not lose him. These women may be deeply sad and angry because black men don't love them enough, but they don't follow through by making realistic appraisals of exactly what their men do to make them angry. Most of all, they fail to take constructive action to improve the situation.

Some sisters today even mirror the male narcissism and entitlement we women have been grousing about from ever since. They'll force themselves on a man and practically demand a date, then expect an immediate and total capitulation. If the man fails to take their bait right away, these ladies literally lose it!

Going through Changes

Of course, some disturbing social realities have evolved within the black community over the past few decades, and a sister's dream of a positive, lasting relationship with a brother is, in fact, more difficult to achieve today than ever before.

I won't lie—many black men have indeed lost interest in marriage. The men I talk to and counsel tell me all the time that they just don't need the hassles. The "numbers game"—the shortage of available black men that's trumpeted over and over by the media—leads many men to believe that they can have women in their lives whenever they want, and on whatever terms they set. Many men believe this to be true because some sisters are too willing to accept poor treatment. Long-term commitments have become an utterly unnecessary choice.

Again, black women are angry with black men for not committing. Yet they're also in denial to some extent about that refusal to commit. Women complain about how black men treat them, but they just as readily defend "their men" by blaming their irresponsible behavior on the economy and attacks from the white establishment. Most of all, they persist in trying to wrestle a commitment out of the kind of brothers who clearly will never commit.

When Professor Patterson appeared on my radio show, he took black men to task for failing their women. Sisters called in, fuming. To my shock, they were not angry with black men. They were furious at the professor for his honesty. After the show, a friend called to talk, and we agreed that "black women must be the most devoted women in America." They cry about their black men not loving them, deceiving them, and leaving them, but they insist on hanging in there against all hope, waiting for something to change and bring that man around. The result of all this hoping, in spite of too many turns on the same romantic merry-go-round, is frustration, bitter disappointment, and the development of the armor of a bad attitude.

Again, sisters' attitudes don't come about because "men are no good." They develop because these women persist in viewing the problem as created only by men's behavior. These women are unwilling to make a connection between their bad romantic choices and how the relationship pattern created by those choices eventually overwhelms them with emotional issues that they mask with bad attitudes. Those issues usually include how they feel about themselves, about the types of choices they've been making, and their narrow view of their romantic options.

Whenever I counsel a client who is trapped in a Wheel of Misfortune made up of bad relationship experiences, I always ask at some point, "Aren't you at least curious to find out how you got to this point again?" "No," many answer at first. "I never realized I had to make a connection between all that and how I got here. I just want the pain to go away."

Women develop attitudes to defend them from pain and sadness so that they can function on some level. Unfortunately, the same attitude that defends you from pain also acts as a barrier to self-examination and personal growth. The tremendous energy required to block all that painful emotion from your awareness and to act as if you've got it all together leaves no energy for soul-searching and reflecting on cause and effect, for discovering how your choices got you in trouble.

What Are Your Love Patterns?

Over the years, I have discovered that the behavior of women who are trapped in a Wheel of Misfortune usually falls into four basic patterns:

1. The Pity Party–Goer. You feel sorry for yourself all the time, and without realizing it, you keep setting yourself up for relationships with men who keep you chronically angry and sad.

2. The Boomerang. You keep leaving and returning to the same relationship, over and over, even though it has never given you what you really want. You keep hoping, though, that he will change, and you refuse to give up until he does.

3. The Detective. You are in constant search of the Perfect Man, the best man, the macho man, the gorgeous man, the professional man, the well-dressed man, the man with the slamming body, the Prince Charming who will love you so that you can feel lovable. You're like a detective viewing suspects in a lineup. You are trying to identify the one you "suspect" will be perfect enough to fulfill your needs.

4. The Picky Picker. You find a suitable man and then take him apart, piece by piece. He doesn't make enough money, he drives the wrong car, he's bald, too short, and has too much belly. He's the wrong color or shade, he's from the wrong side of town, or he's in the wrong profession.(After all, like everyone else these

days, you want your financial broker.) In the end, no one meets your stringent requirements.

Does your love behavior fall into any of the above patterns? If the answer's yes, you've probably got a big bad attitude standing in your way.

The Urge to Merge

The December 10, 1999, issue of *Hilltop* featured an article by Shatikwa Brown entitled "Daddy's Little Girl: The Pain of a First Love." It includes the following poignant lines:

Most girls cry about losing their first love in high school or college. I lost my first love when I was seven years old and haven't been the same since. My first true love was my dad, and it is sad to say I don't remember much about our times of bliss. Like most other male-female relationships, the disappointments, arguments, and tears are etched much more vividly in my memory. It surprises me that so many of Howard's "finest men" don't understand the dilemmas of the sisters they so proudly and loudly declare as their own. We share in their pain when daddies go, [*sic*] they just don't abandon their sons, they leave their daughters too.

Remember the nasty attitudes and bickering at Hampton? That display masked the same deep and aching need to connect that Shatikwa writes about, even on the part of male students.

Some Hampton guys had asked me why in the hell would they want to date only one woman? What was the point? they wanted to know. "How do you think you're going to develop a decent relationship with anyone?" I countered. "It *isn't* about developing a relationship with anyone!" they chorused. "Why pay for the cow when you can get the milk for free?" After everyone laughed at the old saying that's been passed down through countless generations, one young woman stood up to address the men:

"What do you expect from us? We feel backed into a corner! If we don't do what you want, you leave us. If we do stand our ground and assert our rights, you say we're Sapphires. If we do what you want, we're ho's. Either way, we lose. Then we look around a few days later, and you're with a white, Asian, or Latin woman."

That set off another round of arguing.

"Anyway," another young woman interjected, "you guys don't have all that much going on. You got no car, no money, and no plastic. And we already told you we don't deal with no scrubs."

There it was—the pain of disconnection hastily paved over by the hard, protective shell of bad attitudes.

"Okay, hold up everybody," I said. "Don't you think this emotional behavior in here tonight is at the bottom of the problem between black men and women? That when you gather together, in order to be in control and more powerful, you have to dis each other?"

That got their attention, and I was able to proceed to the meaty part of my talk—intimacy. I wanted them to consider how all the hype and attitude is really about avoiding involvement in a romance in which they might love someone and risk being hurt.

We reached the end of the session, and the staff was trying to scoot me out of the auditorium when a group of guys suddenly rushed the stage. One young man gave me a shy smile, then leaned in close to whisper in my ear, "I couldn't ask this question before or I'd be killed off. I'm in love with a woman and I want to get engaged to her, but she seems afraid to trust me. I want to know how to handle it. We've known each other for three years, and I don't want to lose her after graduation." The next young man asked how he could get this girl he'd been admiring from afar to like him. One by one, they each wanted to know how they could develop a loving connection with a woman. Every one of them was afraid to let "their boys" know how he felt. They didn't want to come across as nice guys, that is, as "soft," weak, and controlled by a woman.

This widespread fear of emotional vulnerability and being perceived by peers as dominated by a female plays a big part in the war between black men and women. Yet a powerful and urgent need for emotional connection runs deep and constant in both genders.

As Shatikwa notes in her essay, that need is fueled for many black women by the image of something they never had or only experienced for the first few years of their life—a loving and present father. The unfulfilled desire for a father's unconditional love can grow increasingly desperate later on in life as it takes the form of a misdirected need to connect with a man. That urge to merge can drive women well into their mature years, sometimes to the point where they become obsessed. I treat many women in my psychotherapy groups who are over fifty-five, even past sixty, and still caught up in playing out this ancient dynamic within every relationship. It's not that they don't attract men. It's that they continue to attract and be attracted to men who are as emotionally unavailable as their fathers and to men who will eventually leave. They do this repeatedly, with one man after another, hoping in vain each time that something will shift and the old hurt over Daddy will be eased. They think that if they switch men, something different will result. They're not aware that if "you keep doing what you've been doing, you keep getting what you've been getting." They don't recognize that repeating the same actions and getting the same bad results only brings frustration, hurt, and bitterness.

The fundamental reason for our inability to make genuine love connections is that nowhere in our society—the school system, family, social community, even the religious community—are we encouraged to develop a strong and healthy internal connection with ourselves. All the emphasis is on externals—behavior, appearance, citizenship, religious standing, accomplishment, income, and other signs of status. Yet without taking the time to discover who you really are and your soul's real needs, you cannot grow emotionally or find any joy within yourself. You certainly can't begin to clear up the internal confusion caused by the mixed messages society sends us. Many of us don't start out to discover what's wrong inside until it's too late. By then, we are usually trying to work it out the hard way by attempting to change the other person instead of ourselves. Again, I can't stress enough the importance of looking within to examine your beliefs and your choices so you can start untangling the chain of thoughts, feelings, and behaviors that get you in trouble. If you do not work on making an inner connection, your chances of establishing a deep, genuine, and lasting relationship with anyone else are slim to none.

Attitude adjustments do not happen instantaneously. You must be willing to commit to a gradual, often challenging process in which you uncover progressively deeper issues, until you finally arrive at the core of your stuff, the core emotional issues that are fueling your attitude.

Getting to your core is like peeling off layers of an onion, and we all know that the more you peel, the more tears you can shed. But if you want to know why you keep getting stuck in the same relationship with different men, you have to peel that onion. You have to get past your attitude to confront your fears and pain and to dismantle your misguided beliefs and fantasies. Once you've completed the "onion process"—moved from feeling stuck and needing to be rescued to owning the stuff at your core—you can reclaim your power and start making clear, positive choices about your life. Your power comes from being brave enough to acknowledge the choices you have made and to assume responsibility for your love problems.

Once you get to the core—your emotional issues—you may even realize that the problem isn't so much that men are reluctant to commit but that you are just as fearful of getting close and intimate as the men!

THE ONION PROCESS

CLAIMING POWER

Taking risks
Empowering the self
Accepting choices

CORE

Facing the realities and fears
Reclaiming self

OWNING THE STUFF

Recalling the past
Identifying support

NEEDING RESCUE

Seeking relief
Feeling pain

FEELING STUCK

Needing answers
Wanting change

Getting to the Core

The Beginning of Self-Discovery

You always
have a choice.

Three

The Seven Attitudes

As you now realize, attitudes mask pain and protect a woman from further suffering and loss, yet this defense actually winds up crippling her quest for romantic fulfillment. In this chapter, we begin looking deeper into each of the seven attitudes, into what types of experiences can provoke a woman to develop these attitudes, and exactly how they contribute to her ultimate undoing. The chapters that follow this one will show you even more examples of how these attitudes express themselves in your love life and virtually every other aspect of your experience.

Attitude One—Rage:
"Don't even try to mess with me."

Women stuck in a phase of rage believe that because they are disappointed and angry, it has to be somebody else's fault. This "nothing ever works for me so everybody's gonna get it" attitude keeps many sisters mired in misery and chronically raging about the crumbs that life seems to offer them. Women consumed with disappointment and rage can detail for you each of the great disappointments in their romantic lives and why the blame for these failures falls squarely on the men. They are completely oblivious to how their own attitude of rage set into motion a self-fulfilling prophecy: they *expect* to be disappointed with each romantic encounter; therefore, they usually *are*. With each unsatisfactory encounter, their depression and hostility increases. These women feel cheated, and what's more, they believe that other women—especially white women, enjoy all the pleasures and options.

My client Mary is a walking, talking demonstration of the "I'm angry—it must be someone else's fault" attitude of rage. She's thirty-five years old and has never married because of the lack of any "decent, God-fearing black men." That makes her furious at the world and everyone in it. Actually, Mary's display of hostility shields her from that nagging inner pain, so it helps to get her through each day. By sparring with any man she encounters, she has a ready defense against confronting the real issue: her fear of losing control of her emotions and getting too close to anyone. Hostility is Mary's defense, but she cannot see that she is not really protecting herself at all.

She is actually creating her own havoc. Her defensive anger always gets in her way, so Mary can never deal with anyone rationally. In fact, whenever life threatens to become peaceful, she actually becomes uncomfortable. Mary has trouble even recognizing harmonious situations, whether at home, at work, or anywhere else. Her daily dramas of screaming and yelling at whoever doesn't conform to her program keeps people from getting too close. At the same time, though, she longs for a close, intimate connection. The frustration of this double bind is what fuels her attitude.

Attitude Two—Control:
"Man, where were you last night?"

Too many black women believe that the only way to win at romance—given the ever-shrinking pool of available black men—is to place a firm foot on a man's neck and keep it there. These are the controllers black men love to label "player haters," and men hate this form of emotional manipulation more than any other female behavior.

Ironically, these women are just as guilty of "playing" as the men they accuse. Controlling women engage in constant games of manipulation designed to keep a man insecure, off-balance, and focused on them, because these women are too insecure to tolerate a romantic relationship between equals. In fact, a controller doesn't even believe such a relationship exists. She justifies her behavior by saying that she is simply flipping the script on the way men have been playing women from ever since. But she's only pulling off the ultimate "I'll get you before you get me" maneuver. The unfortunate result of all this gamesmanship is nobody wins. Everybody's a loser.

"If he had just told me that he wanted me," the controller weeps in frustration after the collapse of yet another relationship dream, "I wouldn't have to play these silly games!" Despite her keenest strategies, she's lost the game again. Her frustration and anger—including subconscious anger directed at herself—build, because after all the maneuvering, she's still alone.

Carol typifies women with the attitude that control is the

only way to get what they want from a man. In Carol's mind, she has to stay on top of him. As soon as she meets a new prospect, she launches a campaign to make him behave the way she wants. In the beginning, she weaves her web with a presentation of innocence, sensuality, and warmth. The man concludes that here is the perfect woman—sexy, understanding, and accommodating.

Once she thinks she's hooked him (and sometimes this is after only a couple of dates), she moves more aggressively. Carol will make frequent calls to her new male friend to outline all the activities she's planned for the two of them. Never mind his schedule or needs. And she won't call just once. She'll work her cell phone and his beeper to track him down at work, the gym, or anywhere else. If he appears uncooperative, she comes after him with a barely veiled vengeance.

Carol truly believes that if she can gain control over the man and the situation, she won't lose him. She never seems to learn that the more she tries to dominate a man, the greater the chance he will take off.

Attitude Three—Desperation:
"I'm gonna make you love me!"

Many black women believe that the way to get a man—and almost any man will do—is to move fast or come in last, then hang on for dear life, no matter what. In other words, since so few men are available, whenever a desperate woman does meet one, she tries to lock him up pronto by doing everything she can to please him. No matter how badly he treats her or how suspicious his behavior, she stays.

This desperate "I'm gonna make this work no matter what" attitude keeps sisters chasing after dreams that have no chance of coming true. Desperate women will do anything to keep a man. They'll put pride, self-respect, and even personal safety on the line. They'll even stake their life's earnings on a romantic whim. Driven by desperation, they never take time to consider what they are getting back from all the sacrifices. Their low self-esteem forces them to look to others, especially men, for validation. "If he stays with me," a desperate woman reasons, "I must be worthwhile and lovable. But if he leaves me, I must be unworthy of love." This is the reason these women will do anything to keep him from leaving. If someone forces them to confront their actions and take stock of their predicament, desperate women can turn angry . . . very angry. The anger is often followed by depression, once it finally hits home that all their efforts have been in vain. Some women even become suicidal. They fail to comprehend how their own behavior has contributed to their pain and suffering and what they can do to change.

My friend Dottie calls me constantly to complain about how black men always let her down, yet she's made finding a man her full-time job. Whenever she meets a man, she does whatever she thinks is necessary to hold on to him. Whatever the cost—emotional, mental, or financial—she pays it. She foots the bill for deluxe meals out and other entertainment, even for expensive trips. Once, she had to attend a formal affair, so she outfitted her boyfriend of the moment in a tuxedo, rented a car, and paid for the banquet tickets. Like many black women, Dottie also believes that conforming to whatever a man says he desires in a woman will make her more attractive to him. "I can be anyone you want" is her unspoken message. If he's looking for a mother, she'll rattle the pots and pans and play domestic goddess. If he wants a glamour girl, she will buy hair, get plastic surgery, and take any measure to remodel herself into the woman of his dreams. If he says he'd like children someday, she'll secretly plan to get pregnant.

Desperate women such as Dottie fail to realize that these men never know what they really want. Their notion of the ideal woman changes from one day to the next. So while she's busy transforming herself into his perfect lady, he's already moved on to someone else who conforms to that day's flavor.

"But I did whatever he asked me!" Dottie wails every time. She re-created herself into the image of whatever she thought he wanted, catered to his every whim, and even spiffed him up so she could take him out. Of course, he then thought he looked so good that he traded up to a wealthier and more attractive woman. It's happened to Dottie over and over. She's even let a few men move in with her. She once moved clear across the country to chase a man she just knew was in love with her, but who happened to be secretly engaged to someone else. Her desperation blinded her to all the blinking red lights, wailing sirens, and other obvious signs warning her that this man, like the others before him, was not serious-relationship material at all.

I'm often told that certain men can smell a woman's desperation, like a bad perfume. Dottie is a magnet for men with keen noses and shady motives. They use her, then quickly move on. As each of her desperate campaigns for love flounders and then fails, Dottie sinks further into depression and loneliness. Yet the sadder and lonelier she gets, the more desperately she clings to the belief that Prince Charming is waiting out there somewhere, and the more determined she becomes to step up her search.

Attitude Four—Materialism:
"Ain't nothing going on but the rent."

Some women use expensive clothes, jewelry, cars, food, and other external gratification to fill their need for love. And many of these women look for men with deep pockets to buy those high-end items for them. Men call women with this "cash-and-carry" attitude gold diggers. Material girls often appear to others as if they're on top of their game, but women with this attitude may be the saddest of all. They hunt for men with obvious signs of success—the Rolex watch, the fancy car, the condo in the right neighborhood—because they are convinced that all they can get from a man is money and expensive presents. They never even ask for love.

Unfortunately, the ranks of gold diggers seem to be increasing, especially among the younger hip-hop generation.

"These people want money, honey," cultural critic bell hooks stated in the August 29, 1999, *Washington Post*. "When I interviewed Lil' Kim, I asked her, 'Why are your lyrics never about love?' She said, 'Love, what's that?'

"It says so much about this culture that someone from a poor background has a better chance of becoming a millionaire by the time they're thirty than ever knowing love," hooks goes on. "How can they sing about love? They don't have a clue."

Material girls think they can be happy only with a man who gives them *things,* and the more things, the happier they'll be. Unfortunately, many black men are on to this attitude, and they play it for all it's worth. Men with short pockets will flash fake business cards, lease fancy cars they can't afford, and run their credit cards up to the hilt, just to dazzle a material girl long enough to get her in bed.

I have a client named Roslyn who tells me all the time that men are good for only one thing—purchasing power. Each time she shows up at my office, she's flashing a new bauble. She flatly refuses to date a man who does not wine and dine her and shower her with expensive presents. "If you can't afford to pay my house note," she tells them, "you'll never make it to my bedroom." Roslyn measures love and commitment with a calculator.

Roslyn gave up on men and love a long time ago, when she was twelve and her father left the home, never to contact her again. Her unhappy romantic history as a teenager reinforced the childhood lesson that black men don't bring their hearts into relationships. So, she decided that she wouldn't bring her heart into it either. Roslyn is still unaware that her gold digging is a cover for her profound sadness and hopelessness. She honestly believes that she's devised an effective screening technique to weed out the good men from the bad. As for those sisters who moan and groan about black men's bad behavior, her pity is shaded with contempt. Roslyn's relationship theory is brutally simple: "Get what you can, then move on." She applies literal truth to the old adage "No romance without finance."

Attitude Five—Mothering:
"Come to Momma, baby."

The woman who mothers a man strikes a hidden bargain: "I'll rescue you. (Then you'll rescue me.)" She thinks the only way to get her piece of the American dream—the husband, the white picket fence, the 2.5 children—is to present herself as a zone of comfort for men who obviously need to be rescued. Women who become pen pals and stabilizing forces for incarcerated men are the extreme example of this attitude. Writing leads to visiting, then to gifts, money, and often to becoming advocates for their release. Some women will even marry these men while they're in prison. The women do perform an emotional rescue: the man waits for the letters and makes the collect calls, and that caring presence helps him tolerate an intolerable situation. If the woman is also able to help him secure a release from prison, then all his needs are met.

The problem is that mommas wrongly assume that they've won the man's lifelong gratitude and commitment. That's the hidden part of the bargain, and it's a misguided fantasy at best, because the men rarely deliver. Once they taste freedom, they rarely stay.

More typically, the needy man is coming out of a troubled marriage, suffering from drug or alcohol addiction, or he's unemployed. He deliberately presents himself as innocuous and charmingly needy. Women who are afraid to take a chance with an independent man who's got his business straight find needy men overwhelmingly appealing. "He needs me," they think. "If I take care of him with sex, great meals, understanding, and a little financial investment, he'll learn to love me."

Regina, an attorney with a prominent law firm, was closing in on her forty-fifth birthday and beginning to panic over the possibility that she might never get married. In her mind, the window of opportunity was slamming down fast. Regina had a child from a previous relationship, but she wanted the ultimate—a real family.

One day, an attractive younger man walked into her office seeking legal advice. She listened to his tale of a business deal turned sour and found herself drawn to this man sixteen years her junior. She suggested a second meeting over dinner.

Two days later, they were gazing at each other across a table lit by soft candlelight, and Gary was pouring out his heart about how progressive his deal could be if only he could find the right investors. But the banks wouldn't give him a loan, his family dismissed him as a dreamer, and his friends had cut him off long ago because they were "too timid" to take the risk. Regina was sympathetic. More to the point, though, she hoped Gary liked her. The next time they met was purely social.

A heavy romance ensued. Three or four months later, Gary moved in and began playing surrogate father to Regina's teenage son. Of course, she was now Gary's financial backer.

Everything looked rosy from her perspective, so Regina began pushing for marriage. Gary stalled by pleading his lack of financial solvency, but Regina kept pressing. Finally, they eloped, despite her fantasies about a big church wedding. Soon after, Gary began taking one business trip after another. Regina never knew exactly where he was, with whom, or when he was coming home. One night, while looking for a pen in his briefcase, she found a note from a woman who was obviously not a business acquaintance. She was devastated and hurt. All her sacrifices to rescue this man had been repaid with the ultimate betrayal. Regina's young husband had not kept his end of the bargain he'd unknowingly struck with her. The rescuing was supposed to work both ways.

Attitude Six—Shame:
"Without a man, I'm nothing."

The women's movement was supposed to liberate minds, but no matter how successful modern sisters are in the workplace, most still feel like failures if they can't point to "my man" before the world. Many black families harass a single woman about finding a husband because our community still believes that no matter how accomplished a woman may be, if she's without a man, she is a sorry spectacle indeed.

You may be convinced that this "without a man, I'm nothing" attitude is old-fashioned, that single women are now an accepted part of our culture. Single women are certainly part of our culture, but they are still not fully accepted. I hear women expressing shame over their single state nearly every day, and that shame is a legacy that's still being handed down from generation to generation: "A decent woman has a man. If you deal with more than one man, you are indecent."

That chorus of elderly female relatives responds to the unmarried woman's description of her latest promotion with "Yeah, but did you get that man yet?"

Many women tell me how much they dread visits home

because as soon as they set a foot in the door, they're bombarded with questions about their single state. A woman named Paulette recently confided that she actually feared family visits, especially big family reunions, because throughout the entire week with her family, she'd keep hearing, "Where is that husband?" The pressure had become so bad that she avoided visits home, pleading work projects she couldn't leave, even though she longed to see her family.

Women like Paulette are ashamed to be single because society still dictates that young girls can be educated, but they must also ready themselves for their *real* vocation—a lifetime partnership with a man. Their manless state is viewed as a kind of indictment, a sign that something is missing, that in society's eyes they are "not enough woman."

Black women get this message along with everyone else. In fact, the messages black women receive are even more confusing. Marriage is presented as the ideal. At the same time, they also hear, "Girl, get your education, because the only person you can ever depend on is yourself!" The Christian community chimes in with its own admonition that a "good, respecting" woman is protected by and loyal to one man. And to add to this mess, black men are treated like prize commodities. If a single woman's girlfriend spies an eligible "good" man, she will strongly urge that single friend to pursue him before someone else does: "Girl! Are you out of your mind? You better grab him and work with him while you can!"

No wonder so many single sisters tell me they hate going out alone in public to restaurants, concerts, even to a movie or on vacation. They fear, with good reason, that the world will judge them as misfits or undesirables. All this brings on a deep sense of shame and embarrassment. Some single women will even invent a boyfriend and recount little episodes in their relationship to family and friends, just to avoid feeling like a loser.

"I'm nice, I'm educated, and I'm a proper religious woman who is respectful to others," a client told me the other day. "What's wrong with me? Why can't I find a man?"

The nagging feeling that "something's wrong with me" eventually leads to guilt, and guilt inevitably creates resentment. Resentment builds and builds until it results in an attitude that spews out all that anger and hurt onto innocent people. In the eyes of the world, the woman is cranky, irritable, sulky, withdrawn, or just plain miserable—in short, a sour old maid.

Attitude Seven—Cynicism:
"All men are sorry."

Given the large number of men missing from black families, many little girls grow up without ever experiencing unconditional love from the first man in their life, their father. Even if they grew up surrounded by loving grandfathers and uncles, they never felt the love from that primal figure in their life, the man who brought them into the world. In addition, they never witnessed a model of male-female relationships through their parents. Even if the father was present, he may have related to the mother and/or his daughter in a distant and emotionally detached manner.

These young girls grow up to be women with a distorted idea of a romantic partner and relationships. So they make up an ideal partner who embodies all the characteristics they wish they'd experienced in their father. Their perfect partner can't have flaws. He must be handsome, strong, enduring, faithful, loving, drive the right car, wear the right clothes, sport the right shoes, and be the right skin color.

"Buff and brown" is one of my client's terms for her favorite type of hard body. One night in a therapy session, Sharon surprised me by announcing that she was dating "the nicest man I ever met."

"That's great!" I enthused.

She wrinkled her nose and sucked her teeth in response.

"What's the matter?" I asked.

"He's kinda on the plump and short side."

I asked if he was very short and obese.

"Not really."

"You're not going to eliminate him because of a few extra pounds and missing inches . . ."

"Well, I don't know. He's just not my body type."

Ironically, the woman who makes unrealistic demands for perfection suffers from extreme self-doubt that comes from the childhood belief that "I must not be enough if Daddy didn't stick around." She unconsciously believes that if she were ever to find the ideal partner, she would be released from her deep-seated feelings of inadequacy. This perfect man would act like a mirror to reassure her that she is lovable: "If he stays with me, I'm all right." Yet even the love of a perfect man could never be enough because she'd still be plagued by doubts: "Why would the perfect man want imperfect me? Daddy didn't want me."

Ultimately, the fantasy of the perfect man—who doesn't

exist—serves to defend her from ever finding a genuine relationship that would provoke her primal fear that because Daddy left, no other man will stay either.

As young girls, some cynical women also witnessed the older women in their families relating to men with disrespect and sarcasm. They learned from those role models that all black men are dogs and that they will never get it together and come through for black women. After these girls grow up, repeated failures to find Prince Charming reinforce the original script that was played out in front of them as children. Eventually, they become as doubtful, discouraged, and cynical as their grandmothers and mothers.

Strangely, many cynical black women seem to equate a front of masculine cool with the perfect man, and they find that coolness irresistible. They don't realize that the appearance of elusive cool is little more than a reminder of their father's absence or his distant behavior. It acts like a trigger setting off their childhood longings to be loved by Daddy. Yet that smooth, cool demeanor is often a sign that a man represses his emotions. A woman may get plenty of sexual heat from the cool man, but she won't get warm emotional loving, so the wound inflicted by the absent father will remain unhealed.

Repeated bouts with "cool" men leave women so overwhelmed with pain that they can turn profoundly bitter and cynical. Of course, all this time that they've been acting out their childhood loss with one unavailable man after another, they've been rejecting men who were available but much less alluringly cool.

Clara Mae, age fifty, was a cynical perfectionist who "kept

to her standards." She'd been going with Chuck for fifteen years. He was married, but he made sure Clara Mae dangled on his line by making her promises he had no intention of fulfilling. When Clara Mae was introduced to Roland at a church fund-raiser one afternoon, he seemed nice. She wasn't bowled over by any means, but he was pleasant. After they'd spent some time eating and chatting about the church event, Roland suggested that he'd like to come courting. She reluctantly accepted. A few days later, Roland called. By that time, Clara Mae was less inspired to see him because a friend of hers had pointed out that he was short and stocky and drove an old hooptie (a pickup truck). Actually, when she really thought about it, Roland did not fit her specifications for a man at all. She had always dreamed of a tall, dark, stately man—the image, in fact, of the father she'd always imagined but had never met. At best, this ideal man would show up in a fancy BMW—at the very least, in a high-end American car. Anyway, Chuck, her married lover, drove a Cadillac.

Clara Mae did go out with Roland, but, by then, she'd talked herself out of him. Discouraged by her coldness, Roland backed off. Not long after, Clara Mae heard through the church grapevine that he was dating another sister in the congregation. A year later, Clara was still hanging on to her belief that Chuck, who was only seeing her a few times a month by now, was about to leave his wife. Meanwhile, Roland and this other woman were engaged. Clara Mae was still waiting for Prince Charming to ride to the rescue, while the other woman had herself a nice, solid, hardworking, religious husband.

Got Issues?—The Seven Attitudes

At this point, you're probably starting to explore where you might fit in the attitude picture. As I mentioned earlier, attitudes develop from repeated disappointments and pain that create an inner sense of emptiness and overwhelming longing. The numbers game, the "shoulds and oughts" imposed by the community and your girlfriends, and your own history, all compound that pain, causing many of you to feel helpless about the possibility of change. The notion that things will never change for you aggravates your enormous frustration, which then results in an intense resentment. Those of you who have remained socially active for many, many years can also experience great fear because of this belief that nothing will ever change. Again, attitudes develop as a defense from all this pain, frustration, and resentment. The issues that lead women to develop an attitude are many and various, and they can erode her positive sense of self.

We're all born innocent, with no concept of self, of who we are. Obviously, our differing childhood experiences and the messages we receive from those closest to us—especially family members—affect our self-image and our sense of worth as people. As we grow and interact in our social world—at school, clubs, work, and church—we begin experiencing important relationships with girlfriends and boyfriends and adults. Those relationships further influence our images of ourselves.

Messages about skin color, features, hair texture, body size and shape, tell us who we are and often reinforce the general culture's view of what it means to be black and female. Black women not only have to deal with their family's view of who they are, they also have to deal with the world's stereotypical view of them as superwomen or supermammies. They get pressure from all sides to suffer in silence over all their hurt until it finally builds to the point of explosion. As each negative social experience and message further damages a sister's self-esteem, she hides even more behind the defense of an attitude. Of course, her attitude ensures that she will suffer from even more negative relationships, so her self-esteem keeps getting lower and lower. Attitudes may vary in style from woman to woman, but they always affect a woman's sense of self.

Black women are most often found at the lowest point on the economic ladder, held in the least esteem by society, and have the least amount of power. They are often forced to strive for economic achievement without support from family and the men in their lives. At the same time, many women have to care for children on their own. They're independent because they have to be. Yet these women are criticized by their men and families for being too independent! These same family members will seek out an independent woman for emotional rescuing and financial support, then reject her for her bold style and ability to find her place in a racist and competitive world. No wonder black women construct attitudes to shield them not only from further hurt, but also the pain of their own low self-esteem and low self-confidence.

If family and social experiences give you the impression that you are not worthy of love and acceptance, and society is implying the same point of view, you start allowing people to define who you are and how you should think. By the time you grow old enough to try identifying a serious love relationship, your self-esteem is much more vulnerable than it should be to the circumstances of each relationship. Since you already suffer from the negative self-judgments that you've internalized from your family and social environment, any rejection from man—or any behavior you simply *perceive* as rejection—is going to be experienced as an additional and severe blow to your self-esteem.

Let's say your childhood experiences led you to place little value on yourself. If you started dating at age fifteen, by thirty you're probably knee-deep in trouble, unable to distinguish between the awful behaviors you're being subjected to and the awful thoughts you have about yourself.

Since self-esteem is the sum of your core feelings and thoughts about yourself and your worth, it directly affects how you interpret the events around you. If you dislike yourself, you see the world as a threatening place. You tend to react to that threat with defensive, but inappropriate, anger, fear, cynicism, or desperation. In other words, you react to the threat by developing an attitude.

If you suffer from low self-esteem, you are also plagued by low confidence. You believe that you are not worthy of love, and you're convinced that you are powerless to change your life. So you continually place yourself in negative relationships where your emotional needs are not met. As each relationship becomes another wound to your self-esteem, a vicious cycle establishes itself, and you find it increasingly difficult to let go of toxic situations.

The most important fact to remember about self-esteem is, whether it's high or low, self-esteem tends to be a self-fulfilling prophecy. What you believe about your worth and what you deserve directly affects what you get from life. Self-esteem also determines how prepared you are to take risks and create situations that offer emotional security.

Most black women are shocked when I suggest that their real problem is not so much the men in their lives as their own low self-esteem. These women often dress well, carry themselves proudly, have good jobs, and behave like upstanding citizens of the community. But their problem lies within, and they are often completely unaware of it.

These women may claim to be in pursuit of a good man and a loving relationship. But low self-esteem ensures that they will consistently undermine any relationship with genuine potential. On an unconscious level, they are convinced that they don't deserve love. All this leaves the women frustrated, confused, angry, and depressed, and without a clue as to why.

Perhaps you don't even want to think about the subject of self-esteem. You may be tempted to skip over it. *Don't.* Issues of self-esteem are always at the core of any attitude that keeps you from love. Actually, self-esteem affects your life in many ways and far more profoundly than you may have imagined.

The illustration on page 65 shows how your negative relationship patterns and your self-esteem feed into each other in an endless cycle of lost self-respect.

Remember: your beliefs about yourself and what you're willing to adjust shape the course of your life, including your love life.

Could low self-esteem be your issue? Here's a list of its common signs and symptoms. Read it over to see where you may fit in:

The Endless Cycle of Lost Self-Respect

 WHEN A BROTHER
MISTREATS YOU

YOUR SELF-
CONFIDENCE AND
SELF-WORTH
WILL DROP

AND YOU
GIVE UP YOUR
PERSONAL
POWER

 YOU START TO
FEEL PAIN/SHAME
INSIDE

1. Do you often feel like the long-suffering, complaining martyr in a love relationship with a man who constantly fails to deliver? The martyr's payoff is she gets to play the sympathetic-victim role and win attention from others.

2. Are you nagged by a sense of hopelessness based on the conviction that you'll never get what you want from life, including love? If so, you are organizing your life around the belief that nothing good is possible for you, including a good man.

3. Do you find yourself losing your temper frequently over small frustrations and mishaps? That behavior is usually a sign that you feel stuck in a chronically hopeless state.

4. When you look back at your romantic history, do you see nothing but disappointment after disappointment? As a consequence, do you expect each new man to disappoint you as well?

5. Do you believe that you always know what a man is really thinking and what he's all about, even if you just met him? If so, you are putting all the blame for your unhappiness onto the men you've known and tarring every new man you meet with the same brush.

6. Do you often act on the spur of the moment, without thinking through the possible consequences of your actions? If so, you tend to act on impulse instead of considered thought and knowledge, because you place little faith in your own judgment.

7. Do you believe that all brothers are a waste of time and that you can do bad by yourself? If so, you fail to realize that the real culprit may be your own sense of unworthiness that's led you to make less than wise choices in partners.

The above questions may initially raise your hackles. Remember: Your anger is a defense. Ask yourself: What are you defending? As you read on, come back to these questions from time to time. They will help you become more aware of why you've created an attitude and how you can begin to adjust it.

It may seem as if I'm making the sisters all take the weight for black people's relationship troubles. I'm not. The next chapter tells it like it is about brothers who would make any sister want to shout. But you have to take the first step down the road to a happier life and love with the right man, and that first step is about becoming more aware of what keeps sending you down the path to disappointment and unhappiness.

Awareness begins with realizing that if someone does not return your feelings, it is not a reflection of your personal worth. No individual person or group has the power to determine how you feel about yourself unless you give that power to them.

Take back your power by beginning to unravel the connections between your relationships with men and what value you place on yourself.

Choice is the
starting point.
Your life is the
culmination of
all your decisions.

Four

Brothers Who Give
You an Attitude

One afternoon, I had to get from Howard University to downtown Washington, D.C., to sign papers in my attorney's office. I didn't want to worry about parking, so I decided to catch a cab. I was on the wrong side of the street to flag one down, but a taxi stopped anyway. The driver was an African-American man somewhere in middle age.

"I was just about to go off and catch happy hour on the other end of the street," he said, "but I'll take you." I told him I would just run into an office to sign papers and come right out.

"Since I'll be coming back here anyway, I could wait and take you back," he offered.

We reached my destination, and he pulled over to the curb, blocking the entrance to a drive-in ATM. I finished my business in five minutes, and when I returned, a black woman who wanted to drive into the ATM was out of her car, cursing loudly. "You goddamn cabdrivers!" she was screaming, her face screwed in a tight fist. "You think you own the city!"

I climbed hastily into the cab. "My God! What's wrong with her?"

"It's not just what's wrong with *her,*" the cabdriver declared. "It's what's wrong with *all* the sisters. Man, they got attitudes a mile long!"

I laughed. "Whatever do you mean?"

"You got time for a story, lady?"

"Of course. Where else am I going?"

Here's what he told me:

"I was married to a woman for twenty-five years. I loved her but I guess I didn't show it enough to satisfy her. She complained all the time, until finally I said, 'To hell with you. Do what you want.' And she left for a younger man. Keep in mind I had not been out there for years. So I started taking the ladies out. They demanded this; they needed that. They didn't like me pulling up to their house in a cab. They wanted a guy in a suit and a tie." He turned around to look at me. "Do I look like a suit-and-tie type to you?"

I got up the nerve to ask his age.

"I'm fifty-eight," he answered. "But this happened about five years ago. So, I have a whole new way I deal with the sisters now."

I had to hear this! He was on a roll and happy to fill me in:

"I go out to happy hour. If you go between five and seven, it's 'two for one.' I buy them a drink—whatever they want—I talk to them a little bit, and if I'm at a place where you can dance, I may dance with them. If a lady invites me home, I go for a little while, and then I say, 'Good night.'"

He turned around again to check my reaction.

"You must be so lonely," I offered.

"Lonely?" he burst out. "Hell! I got my dog! I'll take a dog over one of these angry sisters any day!

"I can kick back and relax and turn on the TV. My house is quiet. No one's making demands, no one's yelling at me."

I was stunned. "But don't you want a little companionship at night?"

"Lady, let me see if I can get you to understand," he said as if he were breaking it down to a child. "I gave twenty-five years of my best time to this woman. I loved her. But it wasn't enough. No woman will ever get that much of me again."

There it was, the entire sad story encapsulated in one man's tale: a modern tragedy of black man versus black woman. Brothers and sisters wanting to love each other but too afraid, clueless, and defensive to do anything but battle, until one or the other gives up.

Yet my conversation with the cabdriver was a gold mine of insights into why so many black men run from commitment, setting up the conditions for sisters to develop big, bad attitudes.

One of life's saddest truths is that troubled women inevitably hook up with troubled men. Like their female counterparts, troubled men cope with their issues by developing attitudes. These attitudes lead to patterns of behavior that make the sisters want to shout.

When men who make you want to shout and women with attitudes get together, it's on: endless rounds of game-playing and victimizing behaviors keep both sexes off-balance and forever disconnected. Of course, one of the most frustrating games for a woman is to discover that her man's been lying and cheating. Nothing sets off her attitude more swiftly than discovering that she's been sharing the man she thought was hers alone with several other women.

But men use many other behaviors to keep black women at bay. Let's take a good, long look at the kinds of brothers who make women want to shout. These brothers fall into six basic types: Jugglers, Control Freaks, Jive and Bull Artists, Drive-By Lovers, Whiners and Users, and Jungle Fever Victims.

The Men You Meet along the Way

Like sisters with attitude, brothers who make you want to shout are not capable of creating and sustaining a warm, loving relationship. Unfortunately, so many black women want a man, at almost any cost, that they leave themselves open to brothers whose victimizing behaviors are so transparent that I am often amazed that so many sisters fall for them. Here's the lowdown on the typical characters that drive black women crazy:

Jugglers

Jugglers are usually pretty boys who believe their good looks exempt them from having to commit to one woman at a time. Instead, they parcel out their loving among a stable of females, always keeping an eye out for how their stable stacks up against those kept by rival Jugglers. Like a perpetual adolescent, the Juggler spends a great deal of time on superficial self-improvement—grooming his hair and nails and dressing in the latest designs—because he is only capable of superficial relationships. A Juggler's pretty face and buff body often mask a shallow character.

Jugglers are obsessed with avoiding any suggestion of emotional vulnerability, so they are terrified of attachment. In fact, Jugglers often unconsciously assign each woman an automatic cutoff point. The bailout inevitably takes place whenever the woman gets a bit too emotionally connected or starts making too many demands for time and attention.

Jugglers feed off black male shortage stories. They know the numbers game keeps black women off-balance and gives black men an excuse to "handle" as many women as possible. The law of supply and demand works in the Juggler's favor, making him appear to be a commodity worthy of only the highest bidders, as well as a gift that must be shared. Therefore, he expects women to compete for him and serve him. Unfortunately, many women respond to the Juggler's good looks as if he's a drug they must have. Some desperate sisters settle for a womanizing Juggler and put up with the pain of sharing him just to avoid being alone. Those who don't buy into the Juggler's game are shoved aside and reprimanded with the Juggler's motto: "What you won't do for love, baby, somebody else will."

Tony, a thirty-something, committed New York City bachelor, juggles at least five women at any given time and calls each one "sweet baby" so he doesn't get confused. Tony's juggling act began after the trauma of a broken high-school romance. His first love had swept him off his feet, and he was sure they'd be together forever. When his teenage girlfriend announced that she was going away to college in California, Tony was devastated. He never recovered from what he experienced as a profound rejection. He stuffed his pain away in some deep part of himself and vowed that no woman would ever again gain access to his heart.

By the time he met Emma, Tony had worked his way through scores of women and perfected his game plan. He wined and dined Emma at the finest restaurants. He took great efforts to fulfill her erotic desires and drew much satisfaction from knowing that he succeeded. Once Tony sensed that Emma was completely set on having him permanently, he began to distance himself by hinting at his juggling game. Though he never admitted outright to running a stable, he made sure to drop enough clues so Emma would grow suspicious about his faithlessness. When she protested that he was jerking her around, Tony told her in so many words, "I'm hot stuff, a prize, and don't forget that plenty of women want me."

Jugglers like Tony are typically arrogant and narcissistic, which makes their program especially persuasive with Emma and other women whose self-esteem issues make them especially vulnerable to this type. The key to the Juggler's program is reminding the black woman she could be home alone and how lucky she is to have a man at all. At the same time, the Juggler knows that the threat of other women stimulates female competitive behavior. Insecure women such as Emma will feel threatened and hang in there, hoping to emerge victorious, as "the best woman." Some women are so desperate to hold on to a Juggler that they'll tell me, "Better to stay with what I know than take a chance on what I don't know. I see the evidence that he's got other women—the earrings, the panties, the hair left in the trash can. At least I know his game and what he's going to put me through."

Of course, the option to stop playing along and be without a man for a while is totally unacceptable. These women can't deal with that void in their lives. It stirs up too many childhood memories of being neglected and unloved, and that's just too much pain for them to handle. If anyone dares to suggest that taking some time to be alone, without a man, could be a healing and transformational experience, these women are so threatened that they become enraged.

Control Freaks

Black men know that many black women are socialized to believe that their highest calling is to take care of others. In fact, many black families cater to and spoil their males, regardless of their behavior. These indulged boys grow up to be men who manipulate a woman to the point where she is totally focused on taking care of them—with no need or demand being too great. These men also believe that they can take and take, without ever giving back.

The Control Freak is usually demanding and rigid about his expectations, but he can hide his calculating nature with a pleasant, smooth manner. The woman pays a high price for the sweetness, because it never lasts. Women involved with controlling men keep on giving, with no end and only a single guarantee: they will receive nothing in return.

Bobby, a forty-year-old, twice-divorced military brat, had difficulties with relationships because he modeled his behavior with women after his father's. His father was an army colonel who ran his household like a barracks. Bobby's three sisters and his mother were treated as though their sole purpose in this world was to fulfill the father's needs and obey his every order. At times, the entire family felt as if they'd also enlisted in the military. Bobby remembers that he couldn't wait to get out of his father's home.

Ironically, he re-created the same scenario in his own marriage with strict, demanding, and controlling behavior that left no room for negotiation or compromise.

As a good financial provider, Bobby felt he'd earned a yes-woman in his first wife, Rita. He wanted to know when Rita left for work, what time she was coming home, whom she lunched with, and how much, down to each penny, she spent from her share of the budget. She was expected to take care of the house by herself and have a hot dinner prepared every night. On the rare night Rita went out with friends or her extended family, she had to take the beeper and the cell phone so she could check in every forty-five minutes. Of course, Rita eventually rebelled and the marriage fell apart. The same behavior went on during Bobby's second marriage, which lasted only two years.

Bobby eventually found Patricia, who was happy to cater to his demands and submit to his control. This allowed him to feel "more like a man" and "less like a punk," he once told me. Patricia was much more compliant than his ex-wives. She loved Bobby and was convinced that if she wanted a life with him, she couldn't challenge him in any way. She knew that her protests would set off a tirade: "I don't need this shit; there are too many other women out there! I'm gone!" So she hung on, even though all that work and tension to placate him brought her little happiness or emotional gratification. She was too filled with anxiety about possibly upsetting Bobby. Self-doubts and insecurities, not real love, kept Patricia tied to the situation.

Whenever girlfriends asked how she could stand Bobby, she always defended him: "Oh, he's okay, he's really not that bad." Women like Patricia are often depressed, but they adamantly deny their unhappiness, even to themselves. On some level, they're aware that if they ever got in touch with their true feelings, they would have to come to grips with their miserable situation and take corrective action. In other words, they would have to risk making the choice to kick their man to the curb. Instead, they invest a great deal of energy in refusing to see the true horrors of their situation. Anyone who tries to make a dent in that wall of denial is seen as a threat and told off: "You're just trying to mess things up for me. You want to give us problems and break us up!"

Jive and Bull Artists

It's amazing how many women still fall for smooth talk and empty promises. Desperate women are particularly susceptible to a Jive and Bull man, because he's a master lyricist who tells women whatever they want to hear. If a woman says she wants marriage, a Jive and Bull Artist constantly reassures her that he wants the same. I've known men who were so slick and conscienceless that they'd take a woman shopping for a ring they had no intention of buying. Months, even years, go by with plenty of talk and no action. The woman waits, growing more confused and angry every passing day.

When women complain about their frustrations with Jive

and Bull Artists, I always ask, "So why do you put up with it? Why not move on?" Invariably, the women stare back at me in dumbfounded amazement. They'd never even considered any other option but to wait, hope, and pray for the day when he'll finally walk his talk!

Thirty-eight-year-old Benson liked to tell every woman he met that all he ever wanted from life was to settle down and raise a family. He was tired of the dating game, of coming home to only his plants and cat. He even talked about his biological clock. "Yes," he'd admit with a rueful smile, "I have a biological clock too!" Then he'd share his dream of becoming "Daddy" to three or four children. He'd take each woman to a jeweler in New York City's fabled diamond district and have her try on engagement rings as he discussed the grade and cut of each diamond and bargained with the salesperson. After he and the woman had left the store, he'd tell her that he didn't want to buy the ring there. He wanted to shop for a better deal.

Of course, every time he took a woman ring shopping, she'd rush home to phone her parents, sister, and girlfriends so she could tell them about the wonderful ring she'd tried on and how serious Benson was about marriage. Each woman truly believed that as soon as they found the right ring, they'd begin making wedding plans. Yet Benson always begged off from setting a date because he hadn't bought the ring. He wasn't about to be ripped off by these jewelers just because they saw how anxious he was to get engaged! He was going to take his time, because his wife wasn't going to wear a piece of junk on her finger! No, sir! And since they had a lifetime of love to look forward to, what was the rush?

Actually, Benson had barely enough income to support himself, let alone buy extravagant gifts for anyone else. He claimed to be a self-made entrepreneur, but he worked at Macy's during the evening shift and spent his mornings on his computer, trying to start up his so-called Internet business.

As each woman showed signs of impatience, he'd convince her that his business would launch any moment, that the diamond was being shipped in from South Africa, and soon they would look for the neighborhood in which they'd buy a house for their family. Meanwhile, Benson was bouncing rubber checks and dodging angry creditors.

Dazzled by extravagant promises, the lady of the moment would continue to take care of him and keep him sexually satisfied. She couldn't risk letting this prize slip out of her fingers and into the arms of another woman!

Ironically, Benson specialized in successful, hardworking, professional women who were fully capable of buying their own diamond rings and their own homes. Yet that fantasy of a dashing Prince Charming who'd rescue them from loneliness was far more powerful than the many warning signs that Benson was no more than a Jive and Bull Artist. Eventually, when irrefutable proof of his lies stared her in the face, each woman had to confront reality.

One reason why so many otherwise savvy sisters ignore the early warnings is because they, like most women in this country, have bought solidly into the American dream. Many black women want what they assume white women already possess—a husband who supports his wife and children in high style. Again, all females in this society grow up with the message that no matter how high your educational level or how successful your career, you are supposed to wind up with the big prize—the husband.

Black women read the same books and magazines, go to the same movies, see the same television ads, and get the same messages as everyone else. The difference is that those smart black women who fall for the Bensons of the world are also the most likely group to have grown up without father figures. That unfulfilled longing for the love of their father makes them especially vulnerable to Jive and Bull.

Drive-By Lovers

With so many single black women to choose from, some black men believe sex is a great gift to so-called lonely ladies. Drive-By Lovers like to telephone a woman on the spur of the moment and offer to come over. They show up late at night, bearing a bottle of wine or a single rose, and expect to end up in her bed. There's no courtship, no "getting to know you first," and absolutely no interest in building a relationship. Any passion that's stirred up is just for the night, because he's only passing through. Women who fool themselves into expecting drive-by behavior to change set themselves up for bitter disappointment. Unless a woman is okay with that program, settling for a "drive-by" leaves her with the romantic equivalent of a fast-food diet—hot and tasty for the moment, but loaded with empty, nonnutritious calories that erode her health and strength over the long term.

Twenty-eight-year-old Frank's plan for women runs anywhere from a year to eighteen months, during which time he keeps at least two hanging on, waiting for his weekly calls and visits. He's real clear that relationships are nothing but entrapment: you wind up having to account to a woman about where you're going and what you're going to do, or where you've been and what you've done. He isn't into that mess. That's a little too much for Frank.

When Frank identifies a lady he likes, he calls her, almost on cue, about once a week, maybe every Thursday or Friday— never on a Saturday or Sunday—and always late at night. He chats a bit with her, then casually asks, "How about dropping by?" Unlike most Drive-By Lovers, who prefer to make house calls so they can slip in and out more easily, Frank prefers the woman to drop by his place "for a late cocktail." He might add that he has some leftovers for "a little snack." Perhaps he's getting ready to watch one of his favorite shows, and they can enjoy it together. Any excuse will do to get her over there.

Janis invariably dropped everything whenever Frank called, even though it was never before 10 P.M. She lived on Chicago's Eastside, so by the time she drove to the west part of town, where Frank lived, it would be at least ten forty-five. There isn't a whole lot you can do at quarter to eleven, but Janis would go anyway. Frank would greet her with the warmest smile and the biggest hug. He'd take her coat and bag and give her a nice glass of wine. They'd sit in his living room and watch what was left of some TV program and the nightly news. Then Frank would start nibbling on her ear, fondling her breasts, and kissing her lips. "Why don't we get more comfortable?" he'd finally say. "This isn't very relaxing, sitting here on the couch."

High on wine and kisses, Janis would float into the bedroom and onto his bed, where Frank would intensely strip off her clothes while she pawed at his, in this fit of getting at each other. After a few bouts of passionate sex, they'd fall asleep. Yet it always seemed to Janis that just as she was snuggling down into a nice deep sleep in Frank's bed, the alarm would go off. She'd look up and it would be five in the morning! My God! She'd just got to sleep at three and the alarm was ringing already? Meanwhile, Frank would be out of bed, talking about how he had to get himself dressed and shaved and out of the house by seven o'clock for an important meeting. He'd search for Janis's clothes strewn all over the floor and under the bed and rush her into the bathroom to get dressed. Then he'd escort her downstairs and see her off on a dawn drive back to the other side of town. As soon as she was off the block, though, he'd head upstairs to his apartment, climb into bed, and fall back asleep.

Janis finally discovered that Frank had another woman from several states away who was allowed to spend a whole weekend once a month. Janis was just his in-between, local drive-by to get his thing off.

All that time, Janis hoped that if she behaved like a good, compliant girl who didn't complain and gave him great sex, she would eventually win Frank's heart. Frank's heart had nothing to do with it. In fact, as time went on, her value actually declined in his eyes, because Frank's bottom line was to hit it and quit it.

Whiners and Users

These brothers typically show the world a humble, nice-guy demeanor. Yes, I'm down on my luck at the moment, but I'm really a bright, earnest, hardworking guy. It's just that the white man won't give me a break, and to tell the truth, the sisters aren't helping either.

Whiners and Users are not hostile about their situations, just pitiful as they wheedle whatever they can get from susceptible women. Men who constantly complain about their personal problems and use women to solve them are not reckless sexual predators, like Jugglers, Drive-By Lovers, and Jive and Bull Artists. But they do treat sex as a medium of exchange. Sex is a way to deepen a woman's dependency on them and ease their own exaggerated needs for security and nesting.

The man who whines and uses dangles as bait his promise of undying love and commitment, but he never comes up with that return on the woman's investment. If he borrows money from her, he never has enough to pay her back. If he borrows her car, he always returns it with the gas gauge on empty. When she finally realizes that it's not about love but the Benjamins, she either gives him up or complains so much that he moves on to the next victim.

One Whiner and User borrowed his girlfriend's car for months, during which time he accumulated a few hundred dollars' worth of parking tickets. After he'd exhausted all her resources, he simply parked the car somewhere and left town, leaving the girlfriend with no good-bye and in debt to the parking commissioner.

Typically, women who gravitate to these guys clean them up and dress them up so that they're more attractive to the world at large. Armed with a more compelling exterior, the guy often decides he can trade up for a classier woman, that is, one with deeper pockets. Whiners and Users usually work older, well-established women; younger ones can't afford them.

Kevin was a thirty-one-year-old struggling video artist who showed up in Marva's life soon after she'd established herself as partner in a brokerage firm. Her younger years had been taken up with getting an education and establishing a career. Marva was just beginning to realize that she wanted more of a personal life, so Kevin's timing was perfect. They met at a reception for a friend, and by the end of the evening, they'd exchanged cards. Oh, yes, Kevin had business cards, but they were really for his ladies business. A few days later, they talked on the phone for over an hour and made a date.

The relationship rapidly grew intense, and right off the bat, Kevin shared his problems with Marva. His best friend was a paraplegic, his mother had just undergone major surgery, and his ex-girlfriend was taking him to court for back child support.

Marva was a smart woman with a soft heart for a brother's hard-luck stories, no matter how shaky. She felt obligated as a black woman to help the brother sort things out. Besides, her help would keep Kevin around for a while, because he needed all he could get. Marva was more than willing to deal with his neediness. Like other women who've sacrificed their social lives to get ahead professionally, she wanted a man in her life. She believed that as long as Kevin needed her, he'd stay.

Of course, men and women do naturally need each other. "A lot of women today say I don't need no man," says rapper Q-Tip. "But as a black man I need a woman. I need a female, whether it be my woman or best friend or mother." Q-Tip's idea of need is related to emotional fulfillment. Whiners and Users like Kevin will drain a woman dry.

Marva eventually grew weary of Kevin's incessant problems and fed up with constantly having to bail out him, his friends, and his family. She had bought into his program in a big way for a while, because her social skills and emotional development were weak. Men like Kevin can spot that vulnerable element in women like Marva and make it easy for them to fall into a relationship. If Marva had balanced a well-rounded and confident social aspect with her career, she would never have been easy prey for a Kevin.

Jungle Fever Victims

Some men go on about how tired they are of hassling with the sisters. "No matter what I try to do," they complain, "I can't seem to satisfy them. Nothing's ever good enough. Nothing's ever done right or at the right time. It just seems like everything is wrong, including me. So, if I'm all that awful, why don't I take the sisters out of their misery and go where I can be treated like a man and made to feel that I'm on top of my game?"

That place where they can "feel like a man" often translates as women of European, Asian, Latino, or other racial backgrounds. Nothing infuriates black women more. Now there's one less man in the already tiny pool of available black men! Plus, when they take a good look at the women of other races that the men choose, it seems to the sisters as if these women are often the homeliest and least educated! "Here we are, working on ourselves to be the best we can be," they tell me. "We get educated and turn ourselves out, but our men are choosing these shapeless, unattractive women of other races! Why? Please help me understand."

The problem is that the men themselves usually don't understand their jungle fever. Of course, some men choose women of other races simply out of love. Yet I believe that a major reason why some black men only date and marry out-side their race is because they don't have to face their own history in a woman who doesn't share the African-American predicament. Another possible reason is the man may not understand how his personal emotional issues prevent him from forming a healthy relationship with a black woman. So he simply gravitates to what he's heard will be easier. Women of other races are reputed to accommodate a black man's demanding and sexist behavior more readily.

In 1999, PBS television stations broadcast *An American Family*, a documentary series that tracked the long-term marriage between a black man and a white woman and their relationships with their two daughters. My black woman friends and I were appalled at this woman's willingness to endure years of emotional abuse from her self-involved, petulant, alcoholic husband. Black women want so much for black men to stay with them and work it out. But, as they see it, that won't happen as long as men like the husband and father in the documentary take the easy way out. Instead of "working it out," they find a woman of another race who will put up with bad behavior. Black women are also pained and angry because they know very well that if they were to behave in the same way, any self-respecting black man would kick them to the curb in two minutes flat.

Billy was a proud, ambitious man of short stature who was studying for his MBA and working a full-time job when he found himself falling in love with Jennifer. He was not ready to settle down, but he knew he'd found the prize in this beautiful black woman. His solution was to date Jennifer but keep himself from falling too deeply by also dating other women.

Jennifer seemed agreeable, but every now and then, her biological clock would start ticking loudly, and she'd want to know, "Where's this thing going?"

One weekend, her best friend came to town. To this day, Billy doesn't know what happened, but after her girlfriend left, Jennifer was a very different woman. She demanded to know when Billy was going to make a commitment. She insisted on knowing his whereabouts. One evening, she was at his place while he was studying at the library, and she reviewed the messages on his answering machine. The calls from a variety of women—including some who sounded white—made her even more anxious, aggressive, and less tolerant.

Soon after that, Billy came by to say that he was tired of her complaints; it was hard enough struggling to finish school and go to work. He just couldn't take on more stress. They needed to "loosen things up," he said, open up the relationship "officially." Jennifer was so furious that she hurled a vase at him as he went out the door, then ran outside after him and began kicking his car as he tried to drive away.

Days passed without a word from Billy. Jennifer called several times to apologize, but he never called back. A few months later, she heard that Billy was seeing an attractive, blond, white female and, on occasion, a beautiful, olive-skinned Dominican woman. That really made Jennifer feel depressed and insecure.

"They're all alike," she told me. "You want them, you love them, you give them all your precious time. Then they leave you for the so-called American Beauty. Don't you think the reason we have trouble keeping our men is that we can never meet the standards of beauty set up by white America?"

I answered with a firm no. The problem between black men and women is far less about notions of beauty and much more about self-knowledge, mutual understanding, and finding ways to treat each other with respect and humanity.

A recent popular movie, *The Best Man*, portrays a group of male friends struggling with issues of commitment, loyalty, and honesty—both with their women and with each other. Lance, a Bible-thumping, panty-hunting football player, decides that marriage is the surefire cure for his promiscuity. Terrence boasts that he's never met a woman he couldn't bed. Harper, the protagonist and best man, is proud of his two years in a drama-free relationship, but he gets real weak in the knees whenever his long-suffering girlfriend, Robin, mentions the L-word. These men depict a near universal phobia over the prospect of "settling down."

The overriding fear that creates a brother's resistance to commitment is that marriage will be a jail, that he will be robbed of his freedom. Many men are haunted by such questions as these: Is the ideal woman a genuine possibility? Can you have a Madonna and a whore in one woman? Is fidelity possible? Can the bonds of marriage and children compensate for the loss of freedom?

Fight or Flight

"Men see relationships as distractions and energy drainers, rather than power sources," says William July II, in *Brothers, Lust, and Love*. "Some men avoid intimacy because they do not want to be responsive or responsible for their actions.

They're fearful, and not ready for commitment because they're too busy with careers or school to stop and focus on love."

Sigmund Freud, the father of psychoanalysis, provides an even more persuasive explanation for male commitment phobia. He attributed two related and baffling characteristics of the male character, the need to degrade the love object and the inability to be satisfied with one partner, on specific types of emotional repression. Freud believed that one cause of these traits is the need to repress an incestuous attachment to the child's first love object, his mother.

In normal development, a boy's maternal attachment is eventually relinquished during the period of latency, which occurs between the ages of approximately seven to twelve, just before puberty. At that time, the boy transfers his desire for Mother onto his female peers, who he hopes will inspire in him the same tenderness and passion he initially felt toward his mother. But some men remain maternally fixated, permanently attached to their mothers. The problem is that they are not in touch with this attachment, and it sets them up for an inner conflict that's triggered every time the man encounters a woman who stirs up those old feelings of tenderness and passion.

"Where such men love, they have no desire, and where they desire, they cannot love," wrote Freud. In other words, they have to separate love from sex. The two simply cannot come together in their minds.

Freud also believed men's inability to commit results from another psychological phenomenon, the castration complex. The castration complex is provoked by the fear that if a man gets in too deep with a woman, she will either devour him or castrate him, figuratively or even literally, the way Lorena Bobbitt mutilated her abusive, straying husband.

The castration complex first appears during that same latency period when the boy transfers his attachment from Mother onto girls. In fact, the fear of castration is the primary reason the boy disconnects from the maternal attachment and begins identifying more with his father. If the father is in the home and relating in a healthy way to his wife and children, this transition from Mother to girls can be accomplished fairly smoothly. But if the father is emotionally distant or not present at all, the boy is likely to remain attached to his mother and be conflicted about women throughout his adult life. He will need to maintain control over any woman who seems too powerful and threatens him by provoking his love, because she reminds him of his mother. Ironically, the tool for his domination is often the penis, the very organ the man unconsciously fears he will lose!

Again, the biggest part of the problem is that men rarely recognize their underlying fear. Instead, they act it out blindly, over and over, by refusing to settle down with one woman.

The novel *Cheaters,* by Eric Jerome Dickey (Dutton, 1999), offers a good example of the way men act out their fear. In the following passage, Stephan, the protagonist, is making love to Chante when he begins to feel emotionally overwhelmed and panics:

> Infatuation, love, whatever I felt for Chante Marie Ellis was rolling in so fast that stopping it would be like trying to halt a freight train. I wanted to take a scalpel and dissect my emotions. I tried to understand what about

her made me feel this way, but there was no one thing I was drawn to. It was just the things that added up to her being her. And that scared me. This was one reason men see other women. To thin out this feeling.

A little further on in the novel, Stephan talks about losing his virginity at age fifteen and never looking back: "Men aren't supposed to look back," he thinks. "That's what my daddy told me. He said, 'Find them. Fool them. Fuck them. Forget them.'"

Unfortunately, men pass down these gems of the love trade to each successive generation, along with other misguided assumptions about the dangers of falling in love and committing to one woman.

The "fight or flight" response Stephan exhibits is at the core of most male behaviors that make black women want to shout. "Flight or fight" is set off whenever a man senses the threat of danger—that he's about to be smothered, tied down, forced into accountability, and emotionally exposed, all of which leave him too vulnerable.

The games of manipulation that kick in are a defense; they let the woman know that he doesn't really want to be there and she'd better back off. He may get moody, sulky, turn on the TV to watch the game and tune her out, or withdraw in many other possible ways. A favorite method of cutting off communication with a woman is not responding to her phone call or beeper signal. He may even have an affair with another woman just to gain some distance from his own emotions. Or he'll simply leave, run like hell. All these behaviors are motivated by a skewed instinct for survival.

If his response isn't withdrawal, that is, "flight," a man may actually fight. He will prepare to face the enemy—the woman—with an emotional, even physical assault.

In an article that appeared in the September 1994 issue of *Emerge* magazine, titled "The Brutal Truth: Putting Domestic Violence on the Black Agenda," authors Jimmy Briggs and Marcia D. Davis relate the story of a "fighting" man:

> For Rodrick Bingham, it started the day before his college graduation. Something snapped when he saw his girlfriend riding in a car with another man, his best friend. The two were actually looking for Bingham, but the six-foot-tall athlete couldn't hear his girlfriend's explanation and couldn't reason behind his wall of jealousy and anger. The next thing he knew, he landed a blow that dislocated her nose. "I didn't see it as abusive," says Bingham, sixteen years later. "I saw it as doing what I was supposed to do; controlling my woman and controlling the relationship." For the next fourteen years, he used violence, intimidation, and verbal abuse to manage, threaten, and keep his women in line.

Men who walk around with this level of pent-up anger and fear are not just a problem—they are a terrifying and all too real threat to a woman's safety and well-being, even her life. They should be avoided at all cost.

Psychologists suggest that if a man develops the pattern of fight or flight whenever he perceives danger, it eventually becomes difficult for him to distinguish between real and imagined threats. If a man can't tell the difference between reality and his imagination, then virtually every woman he encounters becomes a threat. He's constantly ready to protect himself either by withdrawing, running away, or fighting

In *The Wounded Male,* Steven Farmer addresses this point:

One of the things that certainly creates [flight or fight] is we have these traditional definitions of masculinity which include attributes such as independence, pride, resiliency, self-control, and physical strength. This is precisely the image of the Marlboro Man, and to some extent, these are desirable attributes for boys and girls. But masculinity goes beyond these qualities to stress toughness, competitiveness, aggressiveness, and power. When these attributes are not balanced with an ability to be emotionally open and vulnerable, and levied with a healthy respect for others, they can be dangerous. One danger is that a man can use this aggressiveness and his power to intimidate and manipulate others without regard for their feelings. When a man isn't in touch with his own feelings, it's nearly impossible for him to empathize with anyone else's. Carried out to an extreme, a man could blindly act out his inner rage on others and end up hurting them with his violence. Another pitfall, if a man emphasizes these characteristics at the cost of his emotional life, is that he will cut himself off from others, withdrawing and becoming distant in order to maintain control.

Why They Do You Like They Do

Black women who constantly want to know why black men seem so invested in fight or flight and other behaviors that keep them from making a commitment tend to view the male-female situation from their perspective only. Few sisters stop to consider that many of these puzzling and frustrating male behaviors—like their own bad attitudes—are rooted in personal issues such as self-doubt, mistrust, and self-worth.

Like women with attitudes, some men shut down their feelings to protect themselves from pain and disappointment. All a woman knows is that she can't get to the man's heart. And that just reinforces her attitude.

Tariq is a thirty-three-year-old, African-American, single man I knew casually as a neighbor, who married when he was nineteen and divorced a year later. We had an interesting chat one day about dating and commitment.

"My God, there are a lot of women out there," he observed. "You can stay out there and sow your oats for a very long time. I realize I can't sow my oats forever, but I'm not ready to settle down."

"What do you think the problem is?" I asked.

"Well, you know, traditionally, brothers are raised in a household with nothing but women. We learn early that it's okay to be surrounded by many women. And then you hear all those tall bedroom tales from the older guys, so you want to get out there and do the same."

"Are you seeing a number of women right now?"

"I don't see any reason to change that at the moment."

"Why not?"

"I don't think it's easy to be a one-woman man anymore. It's not that difficult, but the grass is always greener, and I know I'm caught up in that. You know, I spend a lot of time looking at women and making all kinds of judgments about them. Most of the time, I find it more appealing to get in, enjoy, and get out. Besides, I love flirting. I love women. If I see a woman who is attractive, I want to approach her, talk to her, and play with her a little. Often, my flirting turns into a one-night tryst. I like dealing with younger women because they want to hear about my experiences since I'm an older man. It's a real ego trip, I know. They flatter me a lot. They seem in awe of all the things that I've done."

"So, is it more ego boost than raw lust?"

"Well, I think raw lust can only take you so far," Tariq admitted. "Speaking for me, I enjoy the chase more than the act itself. I would get bored with just the act. But the chase is exciting, because it's about meeting someone new. You know, getting to know the person and going through the necessary steps, from A to Z, to get them. This may sound awful, but most of the brothers think this way. A lot of men don't want to commit because they want the freedom to chase this and that. That doesn't make us bad boys. Those are just the choices we make, given where we're at right now."

"Have you ever had a serious relationship?" I asked.

"Yes, with an older woman. I found her very exciting. She was attractive, married, and her husband worked three jobs, so she was basically neglected. He left her home alone a lot. Honestly, we started out as friends, I never meant for it to be more than that, but she really turned me on. One night, I invited her to my place after we'd gone to dinner, and before we knew it, we were in bed together. It was the baddest stuff I'd ever had. My God, she took me to places I'd never been before. She left early in the morning because she had to get home before her husband did, and I promised myself I'd never do it again. But this thing went on for about three months. I thought, 'I've got to give this up,' because a friend told me that her husband was a government DEA agent and licensed to carry a gun. 'Man, you gotta give that up,' my friend said, 'That guy's gonna blow you away!' The strangest thing was that I had the hardest time letting her go. The intimacy with her was almost like a drug. The phrase I used when I described this woman was that it felt like 'crack-cocaine booty' with her. I couldn't withdraw. I was addicted. I finally understood for the first time in my life why guys put their lives on the line for sex. Sometimes you don't even have anything else in common with a woman. It's just about the sex."

"I thought you said you were in love with her!"

Tariq thought for a moment, then admitted, "Well, I guess it wasn't love after all. I got somebody who feels that way about me now. She is mad for me. I like her; she's really nice, but she's a little bit too needy, wants to spend too much time with me, and keeps talking about marriage. I ain't into the marriage business. I don't know what to do. I see a couple of other women on the side, and I keep her as my mainstay. But she gets in the way sometimes when I have a friend coming in from out of town, and I don't know how to get rid of her. I tell her I have a business buddy visiting, and she gets mad because the business buddy happens to be female. I tell her that I'm sleeping in my room and my buddy takes the couch, but she doesn't believe me. I guess she's right, because I do sleep with these women. Then again, I do have another female buddy I won't sleep with. We've been tight for years. I can go over to her house and snuggle in her bed, but I get my butt out of there before anything happens. I don't want to go there, because the feelings are too strong. I don't need to get caught in a trap. It's too much responsibility and too much drama."

"Aren't you really into manipulating women by leading them on, then pulling away?" I persisted. "Isn't it true that you don't let them know that they can't have total access to you?"

"Well, I wouldn't call it that."

"I can see why you wouldn't want to call it that."

"Oh, you women are all alike." Now Tariq was pulling me into it! "You only want to see things your way."

"It's difficult for you to see what you're doing because the only way you can trust yourself with a woman is by having it all your way."

He laughed, but I could tell that his laughter masked his anxiety.

When author Nelson George appeared on my radio show to promote his novel *One Woman Short,* the topic of that day's program was "Men Who Can't Love." "You've heard of men like this," I said to George. "They have what's called commitment phobia. They can mouth the words 'I love you,' but when it comes time to either marry up or shut up, they're gone. How do you handle someone with commitment phobia?"

George admitted that his book was autobiographical to some extent and that, in his earlier life, he had been a player. Rodney, the protagonist of his book, has bedded 133 women and never stops to think about commitment until his best buddy, Tim, gets married. The loss of his running partner forces Rodney to question his own inability to make a commitment. He casts back through his romantic history and revisits "the good ones" who got away.

While some men who called the show were clear about their own commitment phobia, most seemed confused. "How do I know if I have it?" they wanted to know.

George stated that for many men, commitment means loss rather than gain. One, it robs them of the freedom to be with their boys anytime they want. Two, it forces them to be accountable to their partner, which translates as being tied down. I told George that all this reminded me of the Great Houdini, the legendary escape artist who couldn't be tied down, no matter how strong the ropes or chains that bound him. Ironically, Houdini-type men will pursue a woman until she's caught. Once they've got her, though, their commitment aversion kicks in.

In fact, commitment-phobic brothers are the planet's master seducers. Here are a few of the most common lines they use to woo a woman and disguise their reluctance to commit. Read them and be warned:

"I'm not looking for a relationship right now."
What he really means is "I don't want to have a relationship with *you*."

"I'm looking to settle down. I just need to find the 'right' woman to be my wife and mother to my children."
Actually, he's been "looking" for Ms. Right for twenty years and she's still nowhere in sight.

"I've got an aging mother to take care of. It's hard to find the time to get out and have fun, and whenever I can do that, it's precious. I gotta make the most of it because I haven't had the time for much sex."

Actually, his mother lives on her own quite nicely; she's healthy and mobile.

"I'm too drunk to drive home. I just need to come in for a cup of coffee and put my head down for a few."

An obvious ruse to get inside your place and into your bed. He may even live a few doors down the street.

"I'm about to sign a contract for six figures with the NBA and I wish I had a wife to share all this with."

He does shoot hoops most Saturday mornings, but no one has scouted him for a pro team yet.

"I've got my own consulting business. Here's my card."

The business cards are either a front for a non-existent business or his shady lady business.

"I'm going to turn you out, baby!"

Trust me. The more they brag, the less you can expect in the way of satisfaction.

"I really need some female company. I'm not seeing anyone right now and I'm pretty lonely."

Uh-huh. That girlfriend has been around so long that she doesn't even count.

"You are the most wonderful woman in the world. I feel that I've met my soul mate."

A few months later, you look around and realize that your pedestal is getting crowded: he's been pitching the same line to every woman he meets.

Now that you've been warned, let's move on to the most commonly stated reasons for the brother's refusal to commit.

Fear of Responsiblity

A recent *BET Tonight* program on the subject of male-female relationships asked male viewers to respond to a poll on the top reason why black men won't commit. At the end of the show, the overwhelming answer from the audience was "not wanting the responsibility."

Herman certainly shied away from that responsibility. When he came to see me, he had just completed his four-year stint in the navy, during which time he'd had lots of women. At first, Herman couldn't wait to become a civilian and settle down. He wanted to marry and have a family. But as soon as he was immersed in civilian life, he decided that there were more beautiful women he could enjoy, and he found it even harder to settle down. He felt as if he'd just walked into a woman store, and he didn't know which one to pick. In fact, he couldn't believe that just a few months ago he had been so marriage-minded.

Women were easy to meet, easy to get, and some were even willing to allow Herman to treat them carelessly. He had an interesting ladies program. He'd start off by saying he just wanted to develop a friendship. With his warm, almost innocent demeanor, it was easy to convince a woman that he was a truly nice guy. Then, when Herman felt she was hooked, he'd make his move. His strategy worked almost all the time, but the last woman had seen through his game. When she realized that he was not serious at all about a monogamous relationship, she busted him out to all the women in their social circle.

Herman was so devastated that he came to me. "No more Mr. Nice Guy," he vowed during our first visit. He was going to treat women as nastily as they treated him. Of course, he missed the fact that his own shaky behavior had set him up.

Many black men, Herman included, are not encouraged by the women who raise them to face the consequences of choices that they make. In other words, they are not taught to become responsible adults. These men are usually taken care of as little boys and never told to respond to the needs of others, including women's. On the other hand, black women raise their daughters with detailed instructions on how to take care of other people so they can become true women. The boy is allowed much more leeway and he is protected, again, because that has been the black woman's historic role. During slavery and Emancipation, the black man couldn't protect himself, so the black woman's continuing guardianship is not so much a conscious decision as an automatic, reflexive response to our life in America.

Herman had been raised without a father in a household that included his grandmother, mother, and three sisters. So he'd learned about being a man from his peers on the street. Black males who grow up on the streets, particularly in a city like Brooklyn, New York, learn early that women are there to serve, rescue, and service them.

As is the case with many black men who were raised without a father, Herman developed the notion that relationships are games in which the object is to develop a plan that allows conquest without the penalty of responsibility.

In the minds of many black men, a succession of senseless sexual conquests equals a relationship. Herman and his ilk reason that the whole thing between black men and women is nothing but a game anyway, and women only want men who measure up sexually and materially. That's fine because he wants single, beautiful, well-educated women with no dependents. What's the problem? Isn't everyone getting a little bit of what he or she wants? Unfortunately, this game has no winners. The women end up feeling used and abused. As for the men, once they're dogged out, they're left feeling rejected and defeated.

Fear of the Love Ball and Chain

I spoke with hundreds of men for this book—career professionals as well as blue-collar workers. During those interviews, they all said the same thing: the prospect of merging emotionally with a woman is the kiss of death to their sense of security. They all spoke of their fear of being overwhelmed by a woman. Each one described an approach to women that was almost exclusively sexually focused, almost instinctively so. The tone I picked up from most of these men as they described their romantic encounters was uniformly compulsive, addictive, and in some cases, even thrill-seeking.

Womanizing is often an attempt to give meaning to an arid existence, a way to take flight from simple boredom by literally screwing one's way through life. Womanizing distracts the man from his underlying emotional emptiness and confusion over love, so he turns his conquests into faceless objects that satisfy the needs of his ego.

These men are woefully out of touch with their true feelings, yet they pride themselves on knowing their "nature" and doing what that "nature" dictates.

This pervasive fear of losing oneself in a woman defeats any prospect of love. The main concern these days, for men and women alike, seems to be protecting oneself from losing emotional control and from the risk of rejection.

A thirty-seven-year-old freelance writer named Allen from Oakland, California, had made it out of the ghetto and into a middle-class lifestyle on the strength of his talent and work. Soon after his first visit to my office, he admitted that he had yet to lose his "ghetto child" mentality. Allen had been divorced eight years ago and was in a two-year, live-in relationship with Avriel. She was five months pregnant when Allen came to see me.

"I'm feeling a lot of pressure," he told me about two months into his therapy. "She wants marriage and I'm not ready for it. I don't know if I'll ever be ready for marriage. All I know is that right now I am where I am. I'm dealing with my life and career. I'm trying to achieve a certain position in the writing field, and I don't think I want to take on one more thing."

"Has it occurred to you that you have already taken on the very large responsibility of raising a child?" I asked.

He shot me a look of surprise. "I'm not worried about that. I've got a job. This child won't have to worry about a thing."

"A child needs more than just material items. You seem to

have difficulty with being available emotionally, and that's what I'm concerned about."

"You want me to know how involved I'm going to be? I can't know that. I haven't been a father before."

"No, you haven't been a father before, but you certainly know about your inability to connect, and that's what we're talking about. For example, you have difficulty committing to anything, even to your therapy. You constantly cancel your appointments and always make other projects a bigger priority. You only seem half-invested in the work on yourself that has to be done here. Let's look at what you think may be making it so difficult for you to commit."

We talked about the fact that Allen had never known his father because he'd left the scene when Allen was a year old. His mother had been with several other men who didn't stick around either, men to whom Allen had become very attached.

"I guess at some point I must have decided why get connected if people aren't going to stay around?" he said. "But now I've got to look at the fact that I'm about to be in the same position as my father. I don't want to do to my child what he did to me. That's really why I'm here with you. I've got to work this through and I'm feeling pressured to do this, because in four more months, I will be a dad."

I asked if anyone had ever made an attempt to know him and if he'd ever let anyone inside.

"Actually, you're probably the first person I've taken that risk with," he admitted. "And during some sessions I'm not sure I even want to let you in. You don't know what it's like to want something so bad and be frightened of it at the same time. I can't lose this woman, and I want to be a good father to this baby. But I'm so afraid of losing them and being rejected. You gotta help me get over that. Please help me."

Allen's plight reflects that of many men who father children outside of a committed relationship or marriage, often with several different women. Allen felt connected to this woman who is about to have his child, but even though his heart was willing, his fears overwhelmed him. The real work with Allen in therapy was helping him establish trust. I did this by presenting the sessions in a consistent, honest, open, and caring way. As he continued experiencing these behaviors through me, he began to believe he could depend upon someone. Eventually, he was able to transfer this trust to a permanent love object, his child's mother.

Allen is typical of many men, black and white, who fear taking on a committed relationship, even—perhaps especially!—with a woman who has had their child. That commitment would be the ultimate trap, and it stirs up even more anxiety about losing control.

Without a Father or a Clue

Perhaps the greatest fallout from the father's absence in black homes is that too many young black men have never learned how to relate to a woman by witnessing a healthy pairing between an adult black man and woman. This sets up the fear that no matter how hard they try to relate to a woman, they will either fail to satisfy her or become helpless under her control, a wimp. This is why these men feel secure only in a relationship based on sex. They may feel guilty about withholding emotional commitment, but their guilt is out-weighed by the greater threat of either failing in the relationship or being overwhelmed.

Brothers with Bad Habits

Not much hope can be offered for a relationship with a substance abuser. Alcohol and drugs anesthetize the user against pain, shame, and other uncomfortable emotions. They also numb the addict to the deep emotions of love and joy. A person who cannot face and work through his emotional issues is completely unavailable for a genuine, lasting, and meaningful relationship. Period. End of story. If a woman chooses to relate to a substance abuser, she is usually acting out her own dependency needs through the role of enabler. This is a lose-lose situation, because neither party can make a love connection unless it's a drama full of noise, crises, tears, and pain. An approach-avoidance dynamic kicks in—where he physically approaches her with deep longing. When she responds by becoming close, he then switches emotionally by pulling away. This dynamic is guaranteed to produce the baddest attitudes.

In most cases, it takes many years for an addicted person to become clean or dry, and there will be cycles of "good" periods and "bad" periods. Attempts to rescue the person do not affect the cycle at all. He usually has to reach bottom to find the impetus within himself that will lead him to seek out and commit to effective treatment. You can be a good friend, but don't go there for a good partner.

Fallout from Racism

The deep psychic wounds inflicted on the black family by slavery and racism are clearly key to the ongoing problems between black men and black women.

In *Brothers on the Mend,* Ernest H. Johnson, Ph.D., writes about the fallout from racism:

> Black women bear the brunt of the ill feelings black men build up from society's treatment, directly when many black men simply refuse to become self-sufficient, and indirectly when their men withhold the full commitment black women yearn for. Instead of seeing society as the enemy, many brothers have worked hard to "verbally murder" black women in an attempt to control and dominate them. Rather than offer support, value, and love to the women in their lives, black men have contributed to an environment that nurtures fear, hate, manipulation, and dishonesty. It is no wonder why both parties are miserable.

I've observed in my counseling groups and public speaking appearances what appears to be mutual disdain between black men and black women, in particular in the way they refer to each other with derogatory terms such as *bitch, ho, dog,* and *scrub.* I hear these slurs on the East Coast, West Coast, in the Midwest and in the South, and out of the mouths of twenty-year-olds as well as sixty-year-olds. Across the board in black America, it's the same dynamic, particularly in the interactions we see within the hip-hop world.

In fact, fallout from racism has made black men ambivalent, at best, about black women. On some level, men resent what they've always needed—from the womb to the grave—because we're there when they are children and we're the ones who take care of them in hospitals and nursing homes. The so-called independence and strength exhibited by black women who take care of every problem and every person become a threat to black men who resent being "robbed of their power."

"If I didn't like you, would I be around you?" some black men offer in defense whenever they act out their resentment.

What does that prove if need, not "like" or "love," keeps him close?

The situation is complex. Black men and women didn't start it, but it has to end with us. Black men are subjected to pain and humiliation from the greater society, and the trickle-down process of that pain and humiliation is affecting our community and families the most.

To cope and keep up with what brothers must do just to survive, they have to push down all that stress and anxiety. Ultimately, though, when a man is alone and safe with his woman, the pent-up anger and shame floods him and he lets it out on her. She is not the cause, but she becomes the target. The black man's widespread and sorely mistaken assumption that black women are treated preferentially and are doing better than them in this society is another cause for resentment. U.S. Labor Department's statistics prove that the black woman's American success story is just another tired myth.

In fact, statistics prove that black women across the nation earn less income than black men, white females, and of course, white males. Black women are actually at the bottom of the American economic ladder.

Yes, the larger society has contributed to the destruction of male-female relationships within the black community in that much of the anger expressed within black men's relationships with their families and women is displaced rage over their treatment by the larger society. Yet we need to keep in mind that some black men will use racism as an excuse for their bad behavior. They will even go to the extent of blaming black women for their social conditions and individual dilemmas because they don't want to take responsibility for themselves. They will blame their failures on either the white man or on domineering, demanding sisters who compete with them for power, both within a relationship and at the workplace. Black men are not responsible for racism, but they are certainly responsible for themselves, for their choices and actions.

It's Still on You, Brothers

Slavery has ended, and several social movements have moved on, but some men are still bitter, focused on racism instead of the love and support they could be sharing with black women. The more they blame white society and project their anger, the more tension builds between the sexes. The women and families often pay the greatest price for the black man's hypersensitive reaction to "the Man"—the anger at, mistrust of, and fear of the system. The more social oppression, real or imagined, leads to feelings of depression, the worse those relationships become. Black men tend not to share their pain and anguish with loved ones. Instead, they attempt to present a cool posture of indifference, so the world—and those closest to them—won't know their real pain and struggle. If these men could do the work they need on their emotional issues, they would be able to let go of old hurts and resentments and open up to new opportunities for love and comfort.

It's time for brothers to take responsibility for what they are contributing or failing to contribute to their relationships with their women and children. Living in America is still a hardship for black men. More brothers are in jail and on death row than in college. Police profiling, brutality, and killings reign, and larger numbers of black men than members of any other racial group are unemployed. Ironically, many brothers miss the fact that the black man's greatest potential support is a loving relationship with a special woman. She could not erase racism, but her comfort and support would soften its sting. Like sisters, brothers will only get back from life and love what they are willing to put out.

Black men must overcome their fight-or-flight response, that knee-jerk reaction to their fear of being overpowered and controlled by women. They must start working on their own emotional growth and development, and they must be willing to search out avenues of assistance as part of that process.

Today, many options are available to help black men redirect their stress, anger, and depression, such as the grassroots national organization Concerned Black Men, Inc.

Doug Gilmore, an African-American man in his forties, is a wonderful example of a man who worked on himself to become a more emotionally realized individual.

Doug works as a disc jockey at my station, WHUR in Washington, D.C., and one day, we fell into a discussion on how difficult it is for black men to tap into their anger and express their pain. Doug told me that when he was thirty years old, he had just moved from Los Angeles to Milwaukee and was feeling that he wasn't living at 100 percent.

"I didn't even understand then what it meant to live my life completely," he told me. "But I just didn't feel that I was on top of my game and plugged into life. While I was attending a local meeting in which men could express their emotions in a supportive environment and meet older men who could be role models, a stranger heard me talking about my financial troubles. He offered to send me information about a training adventure. He mentioned that it was influenced partly by the work of Robert Bly, who wrote the book *Iron John,* which was just about to be published at the time."

Iron John laid out a plan that took concrete shape as the Mankind Project, in which men attend workshops where they explore their emotions and connect with older men who act as father figures to replace absent fathers and facilitate the younger men's recovery of emotional vulnerability.

Doug sent for the brochure that describes the project's group encounter meetings. The men meet several times during one year for a week or weekend to work intensively on examining their issues with themselves, their roles as men, the families in which they grew up, and ultimately, with the women in their lives. These intense workshops help the men get out of their heads and into their hearts.

"What fascinated me was the list of quotes from men who had done the training," said Doug. "Their descriptions of it really got to me. They had stopped apologizing for being men, and they felt more connected to the women and children in their lives. One man wrote, 'My relationship with my wife has more honesty and integrity than it ever had before.' It seemed as if the brochure was speaking to me. I was hooked and I wanted to do the training, but I didn't even know how I would pay for it. I didn't have any money. I talked to the guy who sent me the brochure, and he said, 'I believe in this so much that you've got to do it. If you want, I'll lend you the money. You can always pay me back.' "

So Doug went off on a journey of self-discovery.

"I have to tell you," he said, "I did have some fear. Audrey, I've always been the adventurer. My astrologer told me that my archetype is Indiana Jones. 'You're always on the quest to find the Holy Grail,' she said. I guess I'm the kind of guy who likes to live rough and ready. When I told my friends that I was going into the middle of the woods in Wisconsin, a lot of them were highly disturbed. They were afraid I would come back all screwed up. I went anyway, and it was one of the most powerful experiences of my life. It makes you get real, quick! We went through experiences that helped us to take down our guards and begin feeling our pain and shame, so we could begin to sort things out.

"We learn very early as young men that it is inappropriate to express what we really feel in mainstream society. We tend to use what we think are appropriate shields—sex, money, jobs, you know, superficial things."

"And those shields protect you from what?" I asked.

"You know, men are socialized differently from women and we are not taught how to deal with our pain, our emotions. We learn very early that it's better to run from those feelings or to dump them on someone else. I did that throughout most of my relationships. As you get older, you get better at hiding from your emotions and the behavior becomes more ingrained. For most of their lives, men are looking for ways to disguise and medicate and avoid going back to that place where they feel too inadequate to deal with their pain. But you get to a point where those tools don't work as well. Unfortunately, by then most men are completely disconnected from their hearts and trying to live their lives in their heads. That never works. It usually takes some tragedy before a man is forced to deal with all this, and by then, it's overwhelming. That's why a lot of men don't make it through the training. But those who stay are never the same again. The training helps you see that it's okay to be vulnerable. It's okay to be afraid. And you realize that the fear monster has been pushing your buttons from the shadows. It kind of reminds me of the Wizard of Oz. Until you go back and face whatever you believe the monster is and gain victory over it, you won't get unstuck. Once a man can do this, though, he is finally able to experience himself as a whole person."

Doug was so inspired that he brought a number of African-American men together from the Mankind Project and founded Inward Journey, a program designed for black men. He has conducted several training sessions in which black men go through growth experiences modeled after those offered by the Mankind Project. The Inward Journey program is now open to both men and women.

"We need more brothers who are willing to take down their shields and face themselves," says Doug. "Only then will the tension between black men and black women finally ease."

In 1995, Minister Louis Farrakhan of the Nation of Islam

called on America's black men to clean up their acts so that they could respond with love and responsibility to their community, their women, and their children. I was struck by the fact that men who were otherwise uninvolved in the Nation of Islam and Farrakhan's teachings were so moved by the Million Man March that they had to be there. Clearly, they had been longing for direction and a challenge from a black male leader. As a result, the march drew hundreds of thousands of black men to Washington, D.C.

I remember one man who came with his son from whom he'd been estranged for nearly twenty years. The son brought his own son to meet his grandfather for the first time. The invitation was for men only, but many sisters found ways to be invited so they could be part of this historic event as well. The Million Family March, which took place on October 16, 2000, drew the cooperation of such influential black organizations as the Congressional Black Caucus.

Whatever you think of Farrakhan and the Nation of Islam, you have to admit that no one else has called on this nation of black men to take a look at themselves and accept responsibility for their women and children.

Everyone has his reasons for bad behavior, but it's time for black men to stop making excuses and to break up the pity party focused solely on their social predicament. It's time to begin learning from their actions and taking more responsibility for their consequences. It's just too easy for brothers to blame every mess they create on forces outside themselves, such as being born without paternal involvement, economic conditions, white society, and black women's need to control them. All those excuses simply promote more bitterness and pain, leaving them with the weakness of self-loathing rather than self-respect and a sense of empowerment. Just like black women, black men need to become aware of their actions so they can learn and benefit from their experience. In short, brothers must learn to recognize how their choices land them in negative situations. Until they stop looking outside themselves for someone else to blame, that won't happen.

It's Still on You, Sister

The novel *Cheaters* features a female character named Karen. In one scene, she buys a girlfriend a T-shirt for her birthday. The front reads in large, bold letters:

SINGLE BLACK FEMALE: Attractive, gifted, and independent, seeking a mature, honest, supportive, God-fearing, financially stable, physically and mentally fit black man.

But the back warns:

If you are a nonsupportive, no-good, lying, jealous, nagging, broke, unemployed, uneducated, jive, two-timing, two-minute brother, PLEASE DON'T CALL!

Like many sisters, Karen believes that if she just made it real clear from the start that she's not interested in Casanovas, her romantic encounters would become more predictable and satisfying. Women like Karen broadly advertise what behaviors are not acceptable from a man, then leave it at that. They think they don't need to go further, that having been warned at the outset, the man will simply conform. But after this initial show of bravado, the women's blinders often go back in place and he gets to do everything she warned him against.

Letting Them off the Hook

We've covered the major reasons why many black men are unavailable for long-term, committed relationships except for reason number one: *Black women let them off the hook!* They may lay down the law in the beginning, but they fail to follow through in the middle and the end.

Men can have sex without commitment; they can have children without commitment. They can have a woman move in and take care of them without commitment. They can do almost anything they want without committing. *So why should they commit?*

I cannot deny that black women are stuck in a genuine dilemma and that the men know that they have the upper hand because of the numbers game. Women are just as aware as men that brothers have the advantage. This creates a great deal of unhappiness and frustration for women. But instead of taking the logical next step—that is, expanding their choices by opening themselves up to men of different classes, cultures, and races—sisters remain devoted to the men who are not as devoted to them. Black men invite black women to be at their sides to buffer the hardships they endure, but when those women do get their backs, they are too often repaid with disloyalty and betrayal. The sisters accept the tiny scraps a man offers, then complain loudly and bitterly because they can't get more! Why not *ask* for more?

Why not even demand more? These are questions black women don't want to address because they think that these questions are inherently unfair. Brainwashed by the numbers game, discouraged by the harsh realities of the mating scene, and hobbled by emotional issues and low self-esteem, many women are convinced that they have to settle because they simply can't do better. They can't even ask for commitment, fidelity, honesty, respect, tenderness, and understanding.

Check happy hour at any singles' bar, whether it's Republic Gardens in Washington, D.C., the Shark bar in New York, or Ivy's in Oakland, California. The hormonal aroma of intense sexual cruising is heavier than the perfume. The women are poured into tight, short dresses with cleavage bursting out. The makeup and hair are piled on, and the fake nails are painted in bold, attention-getting colors. The guys' pants and shirts reveal every bulging muscle. These are the "beautiful" people demonstrating to each other that "I got something you're gonna want." While the women hope to meet their dream man, the men are hunting for a woman who will give them sex without strings. In fact, if you stand in one of those spots long enough, you'll hear a brother say, "Man, these are some really gorgeous women. I wonder which one won't hassle the hell out of me."

Many of these women show up every Thursday, Friday, and Sunday night, yet they know full well the routine that is inevitably played out. They go anyway, hoping that this will be the night they'll meet Mr. Right. Instead, they leave with their girlfriends and an even heavier burden of disappointment and frustration. Maybe they'll have a few more business cards to add to the collection, and they might actually hear from one of these guys. But in two weeks or so, he's gone and she's back at happy hour. It's always the same.

Keisha is barely over twenty and already addicted to happy hour. A cute, tiny thing with little depth in her scope on the world, Keisha constantly complains during our counseling sessions about being cruised by men in clubs. When I suggested that she take along a male friend to avoid harassment, she answered, "Girl, why bring sand to the beach?"

"What does that mean?" I asked.

"You don't bring a man to a club. You bring a girlfriend. That's the only way you can hunt and be caught. Anyway, the men in clubs will really manhandle you if you're there with a brother."

"What's that all about?"

"They become competitive and then it gets awesome," she explained with her usual dramatic inflections. "Sometimes an argument jumps off! It's too much trouble."

Keisha loves attention, yet when she gets it, she can't handle it. She wants to meet a man and have a real relationship. Yet she represents herself at happy hour as a cute, giggly airhead who doesn't take life seriously, so she invariably attracts men who don't want to get serious. They bother her, she gets annoyed, then scared, and she leaves, only to return the following week because her need for an ego boost bounces her right back into the same scenario.

"What else is out there?" Keisha keeps asking me.

What Else Is Out There?

No one knows exactly what else is out there for you or any other single woman. I do know, though, that hiding behind the mask of a bad attitude, and persisting in doing what you're doing if it's not getting you what you want, keeps you trapped and cut off forever from your chance at real love and happiness.

Whether it's a happy-hour habit, chronic raging at a man because he won't come through, desperately chasing the wrong man, expecting only material gains, mothering a man so he'll reward you with eternal love, attempting to control a man's every move, acting ashamed because you're manless, or hiding your pain behind a tough cynical crust, that close-minded, "What else is out there?" point of view will get you nowhere. It is at the root of all the self-defeating attitudes and behaviors that keep women from realizing their dreams of a healthy, long-term relationship.

"What else is out there?" is based on an ingrained but often unconscious belief that you have no other options. This belief creates an internal sense of hopelessness that leads you to keep making poorly thought-out, bad choices that trap you in an endless loop of disappointment and frustration—the Cycle of Misfortune.

Yes, some black men do make black women want to shout, but good men are out there. Black women need guidelines to help them ease their pain so they can see clearly, beyond the numbers game, beyond their anger, desperation, and other bad attitudes, and beyond that misguided and limited "What else is out there?" Once they gain more self-understanding and awareness of the reasons they've attracted a pattern of negative situations, they can better spot the true possibilities that surround them and make more positive choices. As long as a black woman's attitude keeps her locked in an unhealthy war with black men, she will deny herself access to those good brothers—as well as men of other cultures and races—who truly desire a mutually satisfying, loving, and committed relationship.

In part two we will take a deeper look into the issues that underlie bad attitudes and start discovering how you can adjust them.

PART II

GRATITUDE

Did you know that
taking control of
your thoughts puts
you in charge of
your attitudes?

In this section of the book, you will learn strategies to help you change your attitude from the inside out so you'll be prepared for healthier, happier experiences in life and love. These strategies will show you how to take responsibility for your choices and how to recognize the ones that have landed you in trouble. You will gain deeper understanding of the emotional issues that led to those choices, and how your past experience has been determining what happens to you in the present. You'll open up to new ways of thinking, feeling, and of viewing yourself and your social world, so that the life decisions you make from now on will result from your greater awareness and clarity.

Everything you learn here will help you identify and find the kind of man you really need and want in your life and establish a more compassionate, fulfilling relationship.

Some of these strategies, tips, and techniques can be adapted fairly easily into your life. Others involve more profound changes that require your time, patience, and attention. You will meet women in these pages who are very much like you, and their stories will enlighten, instruct, and support your own growth. As you begin to recognize parts of yourself reflected in them and complete the various exercises and questionnaires designed to increase your insights into yourself and your patterns, you may reexperience strong thoughts and emotions about events you believed were buried in the past. Your emerging new perspective on your personal love and lifestyles will equip you to reevaluate that history. You will also understand better why you've been blocking those painful emotions and issues from your current awareness. You will also begin to see how those blocked emotions and issues have been controlling your life.

Remember: Whatever you repress constantly struggles to be free. It will express itself, sooner or later, and usually in the form of inappropriate and destructive behaviors.

On the other hand, whatever you allow to emerge into the light of your conscious understanding soon loses its power over you and no longer runs your life.

By the time you finish the last page of this book, you will have the insights and self-understanding that create brand-new attitudes, and you will be equipped with the clear-sightedness you need to make more constructive decisions about your life and love.

Some of you may be just starting out on the social scene; others of you may have been out there for a while. Still more of you may be reentering the social scene after divorce or widowhood has ended a lengthy marriage. Whatever your particular situation, you will benefit from the advice and help you will gain here.

As I told you in the beginning of this book, any change—including attitude adjustments—occurs only if you are willing to be challenged, take risks, and remain open throughout the gradual process of self-discovery.

So, let's get started!

Five

Between
the Sheets

I f a sister's love life isn't happening, sex is usually a problem too. In fact, the same attitudes that get women into love trouble also wreak havoc between the sheets.

Sex is a particularly large stumbling block for sisters because the subject is shrouded in the secrecy, shame, and conservatism that characterize our community. The outside world tends to depict us as erotic, hot-blooded, primitive jungle creatures, and black women have suffered from this distorted racist and sexist stereotype throughout our history in America. This is why sisters tend to avoid attempts to openly address, clarify, and develop a comfort level with their sexuality.

Sexually speaking, black women are caught between a rock and a hard place. They are supposed to know everything about their sexuality, but their families tell them little to nothing about sex. As a result, they are not free to admit what they don't know, to seek guidance, or even share their sexual desires with a partner. Black women find themselves silenced by both the black community and the community at large because they don't even have the vocabulary to express their sexuality. They resort either to cold, clinical terms or crude street talk. All this sets them up for trouble in their relationships with men, trouble that ends up being expressed with attitude.

Given the limited understanding of black educators, the church, and families when it comes to the full scope of human sexuality, most black women enter adulthood crippled by sexual ignorance. With insufficient constructive information to guide them, sisters feel compelled to act "as if" they know the real deal. They're forced to guess at what's right, fulfilling, and healthy for them. Some will even pretend they know what's right with their sexual partners.

The truth is that when it comes to sex, sisters want what every woman desires: to be honestly open and comfortable about their sexual rights without suffering a backlash of guilt. Unfortunately, many black women have taken in those distorted and stereotypical views of their sexuality. They are both sexually repressed and confused about what is right for them. No wonder they are frustrated!

Things Are Not Always As They Seem

I remember a man who called my talk show and described himself as a "black Russian," meaning half-Russian, half-African. Ivan said he had been born and raised in Russia and had recently immigrated to the States. At first, he tried to meet African-American women. He found that they presented themselves provocatively, but much to his shock, he soon discovered that American sisters were actually very repressed and uncomfortable about being approached in a sensual way. Ivan's forward approach was natural to him because, in Russia, sexuality is seen as a natural part of life.

"Sex is discussed with children in Russia almost from the point when they can talk and understand," he said. "Of course, as children get older, those discussions are more detailed. They even take place within the family at the dinner table and in social settings. Russian teenagers know more about sexuality than the average American adult. We have no shame in talking about it. No one is labeled. Sex is seen as a healthy way of relating to one another."

Ivan went on to tell me that since he couldn't cope with American sisters, he finally switched to dating international women who live in America. It just seemed easier.

Ivan's impression of African-American women is confirmed by several studies that conclude that black women are less sexually satisfied than white women and women of other races.

The May 29, 2000, issue of *Newsweek* magazine featured a special cover report, "The Science of Women's Sexuality." In an article titled "The Science of Women in Sex," writer John Leland reports on a study correlating sexual dysfunction and race that was conducted by sex researchers Laura Berman and Jennifer Berman. The Berman sisters examined four types of sexual dysfunction: lack of desire, inability to become aroused, lack of orgasm, and pain during sex. They broke the incidence of those four types of dysfunction according to racial groups: white, black, Hispanic, and other. Lack of desire was reported by 29 percent of white women, 30 percent of Hispanic women, 42 percent of "other," and a whooping 44 percent of black women.

Those results are confirmed in an article in the February 22, 1999, edition of *U.S. News,* titled "Not Tonight, Dear," by Wray Herbert. After examining the results of a number of studies, Herbert concludes that blacks—both male and female—experience more sexual dysfunction than whites, and Hispanics less than either group. However, the differences are most striking among the women. Black women are more likely to experience low sexual desire and report less pleasure from sex than white women, while Hispanic women consistently reported the most satisfying sexual experiences.

Why Are Sisters Turned Off?

Why do black women experience lower libido and less sexual satisfaction than women in other racial groups? We've already discussed the black woman's reluctance to claim their sexuality fully, that they've internalized the greater society's racial-sexual prejudice, and several other contributing factors. Another major reason sisters are turned off is that black women struggle constantly with the need to express their sexual interests and desires to their men. A tape seems to be playing in their heads that tells them they have no right to ask for what they want, and their men tend to reinforce this message by the implicit assumption that they know what's best for women in bed. As a result, black women are reluctant to assert themselves sexually; they fear that their men will reject them totally. So they go along with the program and wind up not pleasured, dissatisfied, and frustrated.

This dynamic seems to tie in with another discovery made by the Bermans during interviews with their subjects: that a woman's sexuality is more complex than a man's. Female sexuality tends to be organized as much around the health of a relationship as it is around purely biological drives. That means a woman's sexual desire and satisfaction is as much a product of her emotional state as it is of her physical needs. Since studies also find that black women are less likely to report being in a secure, stable, and emotionally healthy relationship, it's hardly surprising to learn that they are less likely to report feeling sexually satisfied. Black women often describe to me their lack of trust in their men's faithfulness. Since they always feel at risk of being left for another woman, they stay insecure about opening up fully to their man, sexually and emotionally.

Another key sexual issue is the black woman's struggle to relate to her own body. All too often, black women define their sexual boundaries only after they've been violated. Many black women are unaware that it's important to accept and like their body and to be comfortable with it. They know little about how their body functions, and the need to care for, protect, and honor this body.

Black women must learn to give voice to their true self and to set limits that will strengthen their sexual rights. Only when they can stand up and speak out on their own behalf will they be able to draw a clear line between self and others. This ability is usually referred to as sexual assertiveness, which is a way of nurturing and respecting yourself.

When you learn more about your attitudes and feelings, you'll be able to clarify your sexual values within relationships. Guilt about sex is only valid when you act in conflict with *your own* values, not those imposed upon you by society, friends, or family. The next time you feel sexual guilt over a thought or experience, ask yourself, Whose guilt is it, anyway?

Much of black women's lack of sexual desire and satisfaction and their guilt is also tied to the backlash reaction some religious sisters suffer whenever they do become sexual.

"We need to develop another way of looking at sexuality," wrote the Reverend Susan Newman in the article "Sin, Sermons, and Sexuality," which appeared in the Saturday, July 22, 2000, *Washington Post*. The article also quotes from the Reverend David Harkins's address to the National Black Religious Summit IV Sexuality that was held the same year: "Black churches have a complicated history as it relates to speaking about sexuality. Unfortunately, many black clergy deal with sexuality in an intellectually dishonest way." Former U.S. surgeon general Joycelyn Elders was another keynote speaker at the conference. "Many ministers continue to preach about abstinence," she told the group. "But the vows of abstinence can be broken much easier than a latex condom. Sex has enslaved us all. It has enslaved our ministers to the point that we are ready to kick them out of the church if they speak about sex. We have all been enslaved by myths, taboos, and 'isms.' "

The chains of sexual "enslavement" still bind our brains, especially the minds of those men and women who were brought up to believe that sex is dirty and shameful. These women worry too much about what other people will think. Taught by church, family, and community to endure, but never enjoy, sex, many black women who do give in to their nature become overwhelmed by guilt and shame and label themselves "loose." Guilt and shame sow the seeds of self-contempt, and all these toxic psychological conditions erode the sense of entitlement to sexual desire.

We all know that long-term guilt also leads to resentment over having to lug this heavy burden of guilt throughout one's life. Resentment is first cousin to anger, so the guilty, self-doubting woman eventually winds up with an attitude of rage. It gets even messier when you realize that rage is almost always an outward sign of underlying depression. Any sex researcher can tell you that chronic depression inevitably creates sexual dysfunction. So, all this confusion and commotion around a sister's right to enjoy herself sexually winds up as yet another way she gets stuck, this time in a *sexual* Wheel of Misfortune!

Some women are so tired of not having a man and an active sexual life that they just give up altogether. It's too much frustration and trouble! Not long ago, *More,* a magazine for mature women, polled readers on "When was the last time you had sex?" The question was inspired by African-American writer Audrey Edwards's period of celibacy—1,128 sexless days and counting. All types of women, including black women, wrote in and e-mailed from everywhere in the United States. The longest anyone reported being without a man was seventeen years, but most of the women described dry periods lasting from five to six years.

I decided to do a radio show on this interesting theme called "Will I Ever Have Sex Again?" Before we even went on the air, a black woman who works at the radio station ran up to me, waving a sheet of paper and yelling, "I got her beat! I just counted up mine, and I've got twenty-four hundred days. Tell Audrey Edwards to try that on!" After we went on the air, several women called in to report average celibacy periods ranging from five to seven years, but one sister with a Great Big Attitude topped them all.

"I haven't had sex for fourteen years," she announced flatly.

"Well, what are you doing about it?" I asked. She went on and on about how she couldn't meet anybody, that she doesn't like clubs, and besides, she's older.

"Do you go to church?" I finally was able to ask.

"Yes," she answered warily.

"Then why don't you join the singles' ministry?"

She flipped out! "I would never go to church to pick up a man!" she huffed.

That was not what I had recommended, but that's what she heard.

"That's the most sinful thing you could do!" she steamed on. "You're suggesting that I cruise in church, and I'm not doing that!"

She slammed down her phone receiver.

Nothing was wrong with my suggestion, but this woman became defensive whenever anyone mentioned the subjects of men, sex, and relationships. As a result, she couldn't hear my advice clearly. This caller's mind was fixed on an endless loop, telling her over and over that if she placed herself in certain social settings, she was out for sex. What is more, everyone would know it. She'd explained that she didn't go to bars for that very reason, so I'd suggested church for social interaction. But her mind was so closed that she heard me telling her to cruise for men in the house of the Lord. Anyone that sealed off from new possibilities can't even pick up on the interest of a man who's friendly to her at the supermarket or a professional conference. I could practically see this woman marching through life, grim-faced and stiff-backed, never escaping the confines of the box she'd built around herself as protection from other people's judgments and another disappointment in love. Suddenly, fourteen years had gone by with no loving, and she wonders why. But what man wants someone so negative and closed off?

Bad Attitudes in the Bedroom

Not too long ago, my Monday-night women's support group devoted twelve weeks to the topic "Sexuality without Shame." Since so many black women are plagued by a fear of being labeled a "bad girl," "slut," "ho," or "harlot," the group decided to explore their conflicts around the right to accept their sexuality without being persecuted by the judgments of others. We all learned a great deal during those twelve weeks, as each member gradually came to recognize that she was acting out an attitude that had developed over time out of her inner conflicts about social labels, men, love, and sex.

As the group's facilitator, I was fascinated by the stories, statements, and attitudes shared by Lola, Tonya, Aretha, Myra, Marlene, Lillian, and Carla Lee on a range of hot-button sex and love topics, including . . .

- Giving your love to a man who is not committed.
- Putting too much meaning into a one-night stand.

- Being worried that a man will see you as a slut if you have a one-night stand with him.
- Feeling that not having sex for a long time is cruel and unusual punishment for being single.
- Wondering if it's okay while you're waiting for Mr. Right to be sexual with Mr. Almost Right—without involvement or guilt.
- Pulling up on a cute guy in a bar or another public place and not being able to tell if he's straight or bisexual.

Those weekly meetings were about confronting issues related to sexual conflicts and helping each other get through the awesomely tough situation of being single when there's no sign on the horizon of a black man who is willing to commit.

Here's what happened on a memorable night when one woman's experience stirred up a raging conflict of sexual attitudes.

"Good evening, ladies," I said after everyone had arrived. "What's on your mind tonight?"

As always, the women looked around at each other blankly. No one ever wants to go first. Finally, Tonya spoke up:

"Girls, wait till I tell you what I'm dealing with. I met this hunk the other night. He was as big as a linebacker, dark as night, and had the hardest body I'd ever bumped into. I'd stopped by this club for a little while after work. It was a tough week and I wanted to relax. There was the hunk standing in a corner, staring at me, making me feel like I had to do something. So I walked over to get a little closer, and he said, 'Hi.' We got into a conversation. It was light at first, but then I noticed his hand touch my arm a couple of times and then slowly travel from the top of my shoulder down to my elbow. Girls, I felt a stirring inside, like I was about to explode! The next thing I knew my underwear was soaking. It had been so long, I could hardly stand the touch of a man. I wanted to jump him, but all your voices were inside my head, saying, 'Girl, hold up! You don't really know this man!' "

Lola sucked her teeth. "Well, I just think you need to be careful. You don't know who this guy is."

"Yeah," Aretha chimed in aggressively, "you don't know. He could even be gay."

"Don't sound gay to me," Myra said excitedly. "Not with a body like that and a hand so smooth."

"Shut your mouth, girl!" Aretha interrupted. "You weren't there; you don't know. You didn't see the man. Plus, a lot of those hard-body men are gay or swing both ways!"

"If that body was talking to me, it's been so long that I might even ignore his sweet ways, just for the chance to be with him for a while," Myra shot back. "I dream about guys like him every night, and I think I know what it would feel like if I ever met one!"

"Oh, girl, go on and get it!" Marlene told Tonya with a wide smile. "I have a motto: 'A little piece will do you!' Just cover that stuff with some latex, girl! You can't tell what he might be!"

"I don't know how you can even think about doing the nasty if you don't even know if he sleeps with men or women!" Aretha cut in. "That's disgusting!"

"All of you need to be careful," Carla Lee echoed. "Did you hear that a woman was raped last week after she left that new club on the other side of town? So all of you need to watch out!"

"All this feedback is just great," Tonya interjected. "But can I please tell you what happened?"

Tonya had barely got into her story, and everyone's attitudes were already on parade. They finally settled down so Tonya could continue.

"Well, I went ahead and checked him out," she said. "We left the club at about nine o'clock and got something to eat. We sat there and talked, and I asked him a lot of questions. I wanted to know where his head was at, what was his sexual orientation, whether or not he was married—all the important stuff y'all just talked about. And he took the time to do the same with me. We never actually said it to each other, but we sort of sent the message with our eyes that we wanted to be together. So I brought him back to my place and that's when things kind of broke down."

Myra rushed in: "See, I told you, I told you, I told you!"

"Wait, wait, wait!" Tonya shot back. "Before y'all jump to conclusions, let me go on . . . please!"

Everyone shut up.

"I got inside, softened the lights, put on some mood music, and then went in the bedroom to change into something more comfortable. You know I got a lot of Victoria back there. When I came out in one of my little getups, he had taken off his tie, and he asked, 'Do you mind if I take my shoes off?' I said, 'No, make yourself comfortable. Do you want something to drink? Coffee, water, or a nightcap?' He said, 'You know, I probably could use a cup of coffee; I got a long night ahead of me.' 'I certainly hope so,' I thought to myself. I made him the coffee and sat on the couch next to him. Girl, he took two sips and the next thing I knew that great big hard body was all over me. Girl, my hair went all over the place, and my arms and legs wrapped tight around him. I felt like I was caught up in a tornado of thrills and emotions. He was breathing all down my neck and ears, and I was giggling and panting. Then, all of a sudden, he was trying to put it in me. 'Hold up,' I said. 'We haven't had this talk. I don't get off that way. A penis just doesn't do it for me. I need you to use your mouth.' Can you believe he just looked at me? 'My mouth!' he said. 'Yeah,' I said. 'You got a great big beautiful mouth, and I can't believe you don't know what to do with it.' So he said, 'I'm not opposed to this, but, frankly, it ain't my thing, and if we're going to get into it that far, I think both of us should jump in the shower.' 'Excuse me?' I thought, and gave him my hardest 'You can't be talkin' to me!' stare. 'What are you trying to say?' I asked. He said, 'I'm not trying to say anything, honestly, but we could both stand to freshen up a little bit. We've been working hard all day. We just came from a smoky, hot club, and I thought it would be nice for both of us.'

"I could float with that. So I got up, took his hand, and led him to the shower. We got in and sudsed up. He washed me, and I washed him. We kinda made a game out of it, and I have to admit that it actually added to the anticipation. By the time we dried off and went into my bedroom, I was even more excited. I lit the candles all around, found the condoms, and kept the door open so we could hear the music. Then I just threw him down on the bed and eased on down over his face. He was shocked. Girl, can you believe that homeboy didn't have a clue about what he was supposed to do? He just kind of turned his head away and looked embarrassed. 'Haven't you done this before?' I asked. 'I tried it once,' he said. 'It really isn't my thing.' I sat up against the headboard. 'Well, we got a real problem,' I told him. 'I told you already that I can't have an orgasm with a penis. Now I'm willing to make sure you get yours. But when do I get mine? Are you going to sit down to the table or what?' "

Tonya sat back in her chair, folded her arms, and surveyed the room with a triumphant look. She had told this man in no uncertain terms where it was at, and she obviously expected to be applauded for her aggression. The room was silent. Everyone just stared at her.

"What are you ladies feeling and thinking right now?" I asked. Whenever the group is this quiet, I know the wheels are churning. Also, it's helpful for the woman who's just shared to get the group's reaction.

"I'm feeling confused right now," admitted Lola, who tends to be a little unfocused and sometimes doesn't quite comprehend what's going on. "I thought all men knew what to do in bed. We're the ones who are supposed to be uncomfortable and awkward."

"Girl, that ain't even the point," Aretha interjected impatiently. "The point is that Tonya thinks everyone should be on her program. And they don't have to be." She turned to face Tonya.

"I think you were rude and too forceful with the brother," Aretha told Tonya. "You know how sensitive the brothers are, especially about their sex thing. It's the one thing all the men need to feel they got going on. Your style was all wrong and I'm really feeling kind of sorry for him."

"Oh, you're so male-oriented you make me sick!" Myra exclaimed.

"Why are you so angry at me?" Aretha protested.

"I don't know," Myra answered. "I just feel angry and disgusted right now, and by the way, I think Tonya acted like a slut!"

It was time for me to step in: "I think the anger that's going on between Aretha and Myra is misplaced. Myra, you are really angry at Tonya."

Marlene and Lola jumped to Tonya's defense.

"We're always talking about empowering each other in this group," said Lola. "That's what Tonya was doing! I never have the nerve to tell a man what I want or don't want. Instead, I let them do whatever they want, even if I hate it."

"She was *not* empowered," retorted Myra. "She didn't even use her head. She just acted too aggressive for my taste. You can't expect a brother to go down on you when you just met him! They have the right to be careful these days too! There's too much disease going around, and anyway, men don't have to fulfill our sexual expectations. That's their prerogative as men."

"Well, girls, I'd rather switch than fight," Marlene announced. "I found me a nice little white guy. He can at least buy me some gifts, take me on trips, and take the edge off my physical needs. I don't mind if he's not that great at the nasty, as long as he's taking care of my social life and my bank account."

"I don't know what all of you are getting so worked up about," Carla Lee offered. "I gave up on the brothers a long time ago, and after a while you don't even miss the booty."

I cut in again: "It seems to me that the group is struggling with how to help Tonya understand an important behavior pattern, how her choices, both in men and her sexual behaviors that result from those choices, create the outcomes she experiences. I think you're observing that Tonya only thought about what she wanted, with no regard for the man's position. Everyone has rights in relationships—even men. If you want respect, you have to be willing to give it. What we're really talking about here, whether it's Tonya demanding the man perform oral sex, Lola putting up with sexual practices she finds distasteful, or Marlene replacing sex and love with money, are the struggles all of you are going through.

"You really want love, but deep down you're not sure that you are worthy of love. So, you settle instead for sex: 'At least I'll get that,' you think. But even sex becomes a disappointment when it seems as if you can't expect to be pleased by what you want in bed. You can't even get *that* the way you want it. I think your real struggle here is about finding a way to love and respect yourself so you can share more directly and receive what you want. This is not easy for most of you to do, because you really haven't learned how, and you won't admit that to yourself, let alone to this group."

Everyone was listening quietly, with focused attention.

"Some of you act out your emotional issues and longings in the ways in which you relate to men sexually, so you become desperate, frustrated, angry, and ashamed," I went on. "You're in conflict because you're torn between wanting to be sexually sophisticated and on top of things, but when you try to bring it off, you find that you're not really aware of how to do this. You also find that you're not equipped to handle the emotional backlash that often results when you have sex without the attachment, caring, and respect of a healthy relationship. If you can't even handle feedback from this group, how are you going to address feedback from men and others?

"You need to deal first with what's really missing in your life—self-awareness. Sometimes a woman has to figure out if she's really prepared, educationally, emotionally, and socially, for what she's seeking in sex and a relationship. Only then can she make a healthy decision. Some of you seem disturbed because Tonya went to bed with a man she just met. But you have to understand that Tonya is still searching and redefining who she is and what's best for her, and whether or not she's ready to cope with a committed relationship. Sex is all she can handle right now. That's her choice, and she doesn't have to apologize to anyone. Some women are able to distinguish between love and sexual desire. Tonya has clearly decided that during the time she's struggling to find out what she wants and who she is, she's not going to be celibate. That's her decision and her right. It seems some of you are having trouble accepting that she can make a different choice than your own. But Tonya has taken matters into her own hands so she can take care of herself as best she can.

"You're probably also uncomfortable because you sense that Tonya's aggression is not appropriate," I pointed out. "In fact, it's actually a smoke screen to hide her insecurities. I suspect there are other parts of your lives where you would like to make changes. But if those changes are to be healthy and positive, you have to work first on developing more awareness about your sexuality and other aspects of yourself, and learn to trust in yourself. You have to trust that you know what you want and have the right to enjoy it. Only then will you be equipped with true clarity."

"Yeah, but what pissed me off about Tonya was her sexual aggressiveness," Myra chimed in. "She's got too much attitude for me, especially in this group. It's as if she's the only person in the room."

"That's an important point to bring to Tonya's attention," I replied, "especially if she wants to understand how her attitude may get in the way of finding a *good* man. But I also urge all of you to consider that you may be acting out your own conflicts about emotional intimacy through the ways in which you approach your sexuality. Since Tonya is ambivalent about opening up to a man, she tends to act out that fear with tough behavior. That tough act protects her from turning into a marshmallow in case some guy actually gets to her emotionally."

The room quieted as everyone reflected on their individual attitudes.

"How do the rest of you think your attitudes get in the way?" I prompted. "Maybe Tonya is not the only one."

"She's not," Aretha admitted in a soft tone. "I remember one night I wanted a guy to spend more time kissing and fondling me than he really wanted, so I put him out at three A.M. I felt bad after I threw him out, 'cause I really liked him, but I can't stand it when people don't give me what I want. I think I lose a lot of guys that way. I wish I could get that under control."

"Yeah, maybe Tonya was too hard on the man," said Lola, "but still, I'd love to be as clear and direct as her. At least she could tell him what she wanted. Most of us can't even do that. We should be able to speak up for ourselves about whatever we want from a man, not only about sex."

"Why can't you?" I asked, and then I adjourned that night's session. I wanted them to ponder this question during the week.

The confusion and dissatisfaction expressed by the women in that Monday-night group is echoed by many other women I treat clinically. Again, attitudes that represent a woman's love style inevitably play out in her sex life.

Tonya's rage expressed itself in her overly aggressive treatment of the man she had just met and her need to have everything her way. Tonya's self-absorption gets her into a lot of trouble because she simply doesn't make room for anyone else's needs or desires. Men counteract by becoming just as insensitive to her, so the result is a stalemate of self-focused, aggressive attitudes.

At the other extreme, Lola is so desperate to hold on to a man that she will go along with any sexual activity, just to keep him interested. Marlene is more concerned with what's in a man's wallet than his pants or heart. Carla Lee typifies a large and growing segment of black women who have given up on sex and are so cynical about their poor prospects for love that they've actually given up on men altogether.

Sex without Guilt

Tonya may have been overly aggressive and selfish, but her ability to enjoy casual sex without after-pangs of guilt clearly pushed buttons among the group members, for several reasons.

- One, some were envious because deep down they wished they could be as free to make a choice to have sex, ask for what they wanted, and expect to be accommodated.

- Two, some became angry because they don't acknowledge their own needs. Therefore, even they don't know what they want from men.

- Three, some were sad because Tonya's opportunity to be with a man reminded them of their own deep longings.

- Four, some felt shame because this sister was living out the world's stereotypical view of the uncontrolled, sex-crazed black woman.

- Five, many were threatened by Tonya's ability to ask for what she wanted. It forced them to realize that they couldn't do more than complain about what they don't have.

Even though Tonya's aggression was a front for her fears of being overwhelmed by a man, her decision to take the situation into her own hands was basically sound. However, Tonya's other behavior choices were not the best example of how to take responsibility for a situation.

The only appropriate way to assert yourself is to consider the rights of others at the same time that you're taking care of your own needs in a nonoffensive way. You act with self-awareness, regard for others, and are willing to assume full responsibility for the outcome. Tonya blamed her outcome on the man she'd just met because he didn't give her what she wanted. She simply assumed that because he was there, in her home, he was obligated to give her what she demanded.

On the other hand, empowered women accept that the buck stops with them. They know how to assess any situation clearly, and they take direct action to help them get what they want, but they never ignore the other person's needs.

A confident attitude regarding your sexual rights is admirable, but sexual confidence does not come easily to some women, especially black women, because of those societal messages that constantly bombard us. Like it or not, when it comes to women's sexuality, men still have the last word. The double standard sets off sexual confusion and guilt in women plagued with just the slightest insecurity or need for approval from others. As a result, these women cannot evaluate with clarity those situations that could become sexual, and they have trouble asking for what they want without becoming overly aggressive.

Ironically, men are just as confused these days about sexual ethics. They will use the rhetoric of the day about one's rights to express their sexuality. Yet soon after they bed the woman they've been wooing so persistently, they recast her image from siren to slut. Sisters wonder how a man can enjoy a woman so much, yet be so willing the next moment to dismiss her as trash.

It takes a whole lot of sexual wisdom and confidence for women to know their rights in the sexual arena so she doesn't allow those judgments to taint how she feels about herself. Building that educational foundation about sex can be a lifelong job. Ultimately, it's about the old axiom "to each her own." If you feel you are emotionally solid and prepared to take care of yourself within a varied sex life, whose business is it but your own? However, you must be aware and prepared to deal with all the possible judgments and game-playing that could set off your self-condemnations and neurotic sexual guilt. Remember: Guilt only results when you follow other people's judgments and fail to honor your own values.

In the end, to have sex or not to have sex is strictly a personal decision, with no judgments needed. If you decide that you want to be sexual and you can keep clear that sex is all it is, good for you. And if you want to be celibate until Mr. Right comes along, that's fine too. It's "your stuff," no one else's.

It goes without saying that you need to protect your "stuff." In today's society where sexually transmitted diseases or STDs, including HIV and hepatitis C, are rampant among all women, especially sisters, and more and more women are bearing children without partners, it's crucial that you ensure your emotional and physical health. Smart, self-respecting women are responsible, informed, observant, selective, honest, cautious, and protect themselves from pregnancy and STDs. Let's not forget that black women are now the largest group of women infected by HIV and AIDS.

Here's a simple quiz to evaluate your sexual confidence and smarts. Read the following statements and check *yes* or *no* after each one:

1. I sometimes give in to a man's pressure to have sex.
    Yes_____ No_____

2. Sex is too much of a hassle; I've given up on it.
    Yes_____ No_____

3. I sometimes feel ashamed of my sex life.
    Yes_____ No_____

4. I feel guilty after I masturbate.

   Yes_____ No_____

5. I often feel disgusted with myself after I have casual sex.

   Yes_____ No_____

6. I usually do not orgasm during sex.

   Yes_____ No_____

7. I believe I have had too many sexual partners.

   Yes_____ No_____

8. My sex life makes me believe that I'm a "loose" or "bad" person.

   Yes_____ No_____

9. I sometimes have sex when I don't really want to.

   Yes_____ No_____

10. I sometimes engage in sex acts that I really don't want to perform.

    Yes_____ No_____

11. Whenever I want to have sex with a man, I seem to have to tell myself that "it's love."

    Yes_____ No_____

12. I expect exclusivity with a man after I've slept with him.

    Yes_____ No_____

If you answered yes to any of the above questions, you need to correct your sexual arithmetic. You are adding low self-esteem and self-judgments to negative sexual choices and coming up with a pattern of bad relationships that's lowering your self-esteem even further and standing in the way of your desire for a healthy, long-term relationship. And if you care what others would think if they should happen to read your answers to this quiz, then you definitely need to boost your awareness and self-confidence before you participate in sex that's not part of a committed relationship.

Changing Your Sexual Point of View

Phase One: Your Relationship with Yourself

Women typically assume that they are familiar with their own bodies, but in fact, many of us are shockingly ignorant of our body's workings, especially when it comes to sexual anatomy. A good place to begin getting acquainted is by educating yourself with available reading materials. I recommend two helpful and well-known books, *Our Bodies, Ourselves* and *Will the Real Woman Please Stand Up*. You can check the Internet or a bookstore for more titles.

To help you figure out what you don't know about female sexuality, try writing an account of your own sexual history. When you've completed that history, write down whatever you know about your family members' sexual history, especially the women. That can be a real eye-opener, because it will tell you a good deal about how and what you learned about sexuality. This is an essential part of discovering your own sexual voice.

Your body image also plays a key role in how you view

your sexuality. Too many women are uncomfortable with their bodies. Some can't even stand to look at their bodies in the mirror. In effect, they are rejecting their physical selves. The media reinforces this rejection through the implied but clear message that female beauty means young and thin. Black women in search of love feel they have to conform to this stringent ideal of beauty. If they do not measure up to the images of womanhood found in so many magazines, on TV, and on the movie screen, many women conclude that their look is not acceptable. Unfortunately, so many women—especially black and Latino women—spend so many years disliking their body that I've even heard them refer to that body as an "it," as if it's a separate and much-loathed appendage. When it comes to the sexual aspects of those bodies, these women have all kinds of names: *kitty, money box, poontang,* and other terms that help them avoid a proper identification.

If you disown any part of your body, you obviously do not accept yourself completely. If you can't accept yourself, how can you expect someone else to accept you?

It's not surprising, therefore, to learn that most black women react with enormous guilt to the idea of self-pleasuring. Yet those women who are able to accept and learn about their bodies through self-pleasuring are less likely to suffer a split between "I" and their physical selves. Women of all races are not encouraged by this culture to live in their bodies. It's as if their bodies exist only for others to view, lust after, and to enjoy or abuse. Unlike men, who are socialized to live more fully in their bodies, women in this society need to learn about their bodies and how to trust them through accurate knowledge and acquiring the comfort that comes from that information. More trust of the physical self strengthens confidence, self-image, and self-worth.

Sometimes, though, the most intimate experience you can have with yourself is through abstaining from sex for a while. This can help you get in touch with your true sexual values, build self-trust, and rediscover your sexuality. As you can see, sexuality has to do with much more than having sex. It also has to do with how you feel about your body, your spiritual connection to that body, and embracing a total sensuality that involves the many ways in which your body feels pleasure that are not necessarily sexual. That includes the joys of foot, hand, head, or total body massage; a long, luxurious soak in a bubble bath; a walk in the forest or along the seashore on a glorious day; and other simple pleasures of life that are experienced through the body.

Phase Two: Your Relationship with Others

To risk being intimate with another person does not mean jumping into bed with that partner to check him out. In fact, genuine intimacy has to do with sharing other deep, passionate experiences, thoughts, and feelings. Black women who prematurely give up their hopes for a respectful, intimate relationship usually have difficulty making a conscious decision to develop closeness in the first place. They don't know how to develop that emotional closeness, and they're also afraid of it. In other words, you have to do your homework on yourself—strengthen your relationship with yourself—before you can be ready for intimacy with someone else.

Your relationships with others must hinge on mutual respect and self-respect, and this issue is connected closely to defining your sexual boundaries. As I have already noted, all too often, black women learn about their sexual boundaries only after they've been violated through childhood abuse, acquaintance rape, and stranger rape. Unfortunately, black women are the least likely group to report rape, probably because of sexual shame and self-blame. If the rapist is an acquaintance, some women will even remain friends with him to stay in denial about what has happened to them. Many women are even in denial about the fact that someone they know well, are fond of, and even desire on some level could possibly force them to have unwanted sex.

Yet it's essential that you acknowledge and give voice to your true feelings and the limits you must set to be comfortable. Only then can you strengthen your sexual boundaries with others. You must learn to draw a line between self and others by speaking out for yourself. Sexual assertiveness allows you to respect and take care of yourself and raise your self-esteem.

When you allow yourself to experience your true feelings and attitudes about your sexuality, you will become clearer about your sexual value system. One way to do this is to use your reactions of guilt to pinpoint your emotional issues regarding your sexuality and your sexual rights. If you feel only a slight pang of guilt about a sexual question and then move past it, you probably don't have any issue about that aspect of your sexuality. But if you suffer from extreme guilt about saying no, saying yes, or wanting a particular sexual activity, then you know that's where you need to work on clarifying your values. Guilt usually means that you are imposing someone else's values on yourself, whether those values come from society, friends, or family.

You can use the following questions to help you make sexual decisions that are completely your own.

Questions to Ask Yourself before
Jumping into Bed with Him

1. Is this about a relationship or a sexual fling?

2. If it's a sexual fling, am I okay with that?

3. Will my friends and family think less of me if I sleep with him?

4. Will their disapproval make me feel guilty?

5. If I never hear from him again, will I lose self-respect?

Add any other questions you can think of that address your particular issues about your sexuality. Don't forget to go through these questions the next time you're trying to decide whether to sleep with someone.

Every Kiss Is Not a Contract

Because women who lack sexual confidence feel ashamed whenever they have casual sex, they often try to make more of the relationship than it really is. They turn casual sex into a promise. Overwhelmed by their need for approval, they expect any man with whom they have sexual contact to commit to a relationship so these women can live with the fact that they've had casual sex. Therefore, they tell themselves that it's love, when the truth is neither the man or the woman knows right away what their connection is or what it could become. The relationship is new and both parties are checking each other out. They should be either waiting to discover what will happen or simply enjoying the excitement and attraction of the moment. Or, if they can't handle it, they shouldn't be having sex at all.

Still, many sisters insist on treating each sex act like the entry ticket to a relationship. Some even fill their heads with wedding-plan fantasies and visions of an idyllic marriage after only one night with a man.

As one smart person once said, "Women have sex in order to be loved, and men make love in order to have sex."

The sisters' inability to accept sexual enjoyment for its own sake and distinguish between casual sex and a deep relationship founded on love and emotional sharing isn't helped by that much-hyped numbers game and the cutthroat competition between black women. Many sisters feel they have to have an edge. So they try to create that edge by acting like a sexually savvy and willing woman the guy will want to see again and again.

The result is that sex, not love, is being negotiated out there, and many sisters are dressing and presenting themselves to get sexual attention in any possible way. Sex is the top-traded commodity of the day.

Of course, if you use sex to win love, you've created the perfect setup for failure. No one commits to sex alone. Once again, if you find yourself becoming caught up in behaviors that don't create the outcomes you want, you're less likely to find the love and commitment you really long for. Too many women attempt to gain access to a man's heart by doing whatever they think it will take and by trying to make sex more than it really is.

If a sister succumbs to her natural desire for emotional

attachment and talks herself into believing that the man is committed after a few nights of sex, what exactly is happening? She is mistaking sexual excitement for the emotional state of "being in love," and her anxiety can lead her to rash behavior: she'll show up at his door unannounced, bearing food and wine, and become angry if he is unavailable; she'll beep him all night long to check up on his whereabouts. If she discovers where he hangs out, she goes there. She's prepared to move in after the first sexual encounter and becomes hurt if he says no. She's also ready and willing to create a scene if she sees that man with another woman, even though he never said he wanted exclusivity. She's forgotten that every kiss is not a contract, and just 'cause he's sexed you, he's not necessarily "your man."

The overanxious sister becomes angry, depressed, and hurt once she realizes that she's fooled herself yet again into believing that if a man enjoys sex with her—likes her smell and touch and comes back many times for more—he must love her. Wrong! He's in love with the game, the pursuit, and the stuff, and especially, *his own* climactic release. He may seem satisfied and happy about what takes place between the sheets, but that does not mean he wants commitment.

"Sisters gotta understand one thing," a male colleague once told me. "The old saying is true: 'A hard dick has no conscience.' " Even if he comes back many, many times, that still doesn't mean he's falling for you. It's about the stuff.

If you want a serious relationship, consider not giving up your stuff too quickly. A serious relationship is emotionally intimate, genuinely caring, based on mutual goals, long-term, and committed. The unfortunate truth is that many men view an "easy lay" as a poor candidate for a relationship. The rap goes something like this: "She gave in to me so easily, she must be doing it with others." Just because he acts like he wants you to be comfortable about jumping right into bed with him, and it's the new millennium, blah, blah, blah, doesn't mean that his underlying attitude about casual sex and casual sex partners has changed since Granddad's time. Despite all the talk about free sex in this modern era, women are still victimized by the double standard.

I'm not suggesting for a moment that modern sisters should cave in to this injustice and not take care of their physical needs. After all, many black women will remain single most of their life. What's a sister to do? The idea of staying celibate is neither realistic nor necessarily desirable. What is realistic and desirable, though, is learning how to avoid the negative situations that cause you to develop a "bad" attitude and protecting yourself by learning how to spot those brothers who are not interested in a serious relationship. In other words, whenever you do choose to have sex, protect yourself from the obvious dangers—physical and emotional.

Here are a few concrete tips on how to enjoy yourself while taking care of yourself:

1. Know what your potential sexual partner's intentions are before you say yes. Don't assume that you know. In other words, look before you leap into that bed.

2. Remember, just because he tells you he enjoys your body, it doesn't mean he's about to put the ring on your finger.

3. Set the pace for how fast you want matters to go. Be in charge of your own agenda.

4. Is he a vampire who only shows up for nighttime booty calls? If you're a vampire too, fine. But if you thought this was a daytime relationship, don't stay in it, hoping he'll come around. Enjoy those nights or end it right there.

5. If it don't fit, quit. don't force the relationship. Do a reality check first. Listen to what he *doesn't* tell you. Notice what he *doesn't* do. Is he showing the signs of caring and interest in a long-term, committed relationship? Or are you just filling in the blanks yourself?

6. Shut down your one-woman help clinic for commitment-phobic men. Trying to turn them into marriage-minded partners is a waste of your time and energy, and your self-esteem will drop down several notches at least when you fail. This includes those smooth mack daddies. They play into your fantasies; don't you play into his game. But if you want a hair off that dog, take it with no illusions, please.

7. If you're starved for attention, you don't have to use sex to get it. Do something positive and self-enhancing. Take a course, travel, or volunteer at a hospital or some other charitable endeavor that will make you proud of yourself.

8. Sex is best when you feel good about yourself, he feels good about himself, and no one feels pressured to participate because sex is being used as a bargaining chip. Remember: Every erection does not require your emergency treatment.

Low Self-Esteem
+ Negative Sexual Choices

= Bad Relationships

You Make Me Feel
like a Natural Woman

Women who lack confidence and self-esteem also feel empty and incomplete, so they look to others, especially men, to make them feel whole, like a "natural" woman. Their quest for love is always motivated by three powerful but unconscious wishes:

One, the urge to merge with someone "special."

Two, the need to be validated.

Three, the desire to join that wonderful world made up entirely of couples.

These wishes are all fueled by impulses to "get" rather than "give," so they almost always lead to a clash between the woman and the man she expects to fulfill her needs, urges, and desires and make her feel whole and complete.

Early in our development, we experience what psychologists call narcissistic needs—impulses toward self-love and taking care of ourselves. In moderation, narcissistic needs are healthy and natural. They come about through modeling the positive, loving care we should get from our parents. In perceiving that our parents love us, we learn to administer self-love and to soothe ourselves. Through this process, we become less anxious and controlled by urges to merge with others so they can fill our inner needs. We feel complete within ourselves.

Women who seek validation through their lovers are driven by the need to bolster their self-worth and self-love because something was lacking in those primal childhood relationships. Either they never got the message that they were loved and cared for by their parents, or they didn't get enough love and care. So they never learn how to administer that love and care to themselves and achieve a healthy level of independence.

These adults search the world for someone who will provide what they never received and cannot give to themselves. That is why so many black women who grew up in single-parent households or with emotionally distant fathers hold up their sexuality as a bargaining chip for love.

Delores, an attractive, forty-eight-year-old, four-time divorcée, had never known her father. She grew up believing that if she played it easygoing and sexually available, she'd eventually run into the man who would fulfill her dreams of unconditional love. Big mistake.

She met Troy, an attractive, aggressive, young corporate lawyer at a national Black NBA convention held in Detroit. He was equipped with radar for women in emotional need like Delores, and he hunted them down at national black conferences like this one, where females usually outnumber males by five to one. As usual, Troy was decked out in his finest threads, most expensive jewelry, and armed with plenty of business cards—standard booty-hunter equipment.

Troy was just turning a corner in the convention hall when he bumped into Delores, who was dressed to be caught in a skintight red dress and a pair of four-inch high heels. "Damn, she's fine!" he thought. They smiled, spoke, and decided go to the hotel bar for drinks. By the third day of the conference, they were excited about each other. Troy invited Delores to his room after a party and Delores was happy to accept. She believed that "if you satisfy a man's needs, he will want more time with you, and after a while, who knows where that will lead?" Her marriages had failed, and she was tired of the guys she'd been dating back home. Besides, none of them had Troy's economic potential. She was determined to snag him.

After the conference in Detroit ended, Delores went back to Buffalo, New York, and Troy returned to Boston. Delores stayed in touch every day by telephone or e-mail, and Troy did respond, although he sometimes took his time getting back to her. All she could think about was how great he was in bed and how financially solvent he would be in a few years. But Troy had never indicated that his interest went beyond casual sex. Somehow Delores missed the cues he was sending that while he'd enjoyed her for a few days, he was going back to Boston and business as usual.

As Troy showed fewer and fewer signs of interest, Delores grew increasingly confused and anxious. She couldn't figure out what she'd done wrong. "Damn," she thought, "how did I get into something where I feel so out of control? I got to do something!" Her confusion, anxiety, and anger continued to build until she decided a trip to Boston would remind Troy of how much he'd enjoyed her. The next time she was able to reach him by telephone, she announced that she was coming. When he begged off, pleading a heavy load of work, Delores lost it and accused him of leading her on and taking advantage of her.

"Hello! We're both grown-ups and we knew what we were getting into," Troy retorted. "I enjoyed you, but it was for then. I got a life of my own here. I'm trying to make partner, and my work doesn't leave time for a serious relationship." Delores slammed down the receiver and broke into sobs. Then she called her best friend. "They're all alike," she cried to her friend. "They work you until they get it. Once they get it, they're gone!" But deep down, Delores was really angry with herself. After all her experience, she'd allowed herself to forget that sex doesn't come with a promise.

Thirty-year-old Naomi hasn't grasped that lesson yet. She tells me she gets anxious and nervous every time she meets a new man, because she wants so badly to build a real relationship. She is afraid to be alone, so she'll spend time with any man who shows a little interest. Need and fear are her enemies because they prevent her from making real connections. She wants all the pieces to come together, right away, and with every man. Every time they don't, she falls apart. Naomi is simply unable to wait for a relationship to develop naturally, over time. Whenever she meets a man who seems vaguely suitable, the wedding plans go into gear immediately. A few weeks later, Naomi is distraught once again, because the man is not interested in marrying her. Her tales of woe are almost always about wanting something to happen immediately, so her fears and anxieties over being single will be soothed. It never happens within her brief time frame, so Naomi, like a lot of younger women, becomes depressed and dejected. She whines for hours to girlfriends. The friends convince her to go out so she'll feel better: "Girl, get yourself together, throw on some Donna K, and let's go to the Fox Trap and check out some cuties."

It never works. Sure, she'll meet someone else, but she's so depressed over the last failure that she simply makes another impetuous and negative choice and winds up back where she began, having sex and expecting commitment from someone who is clearly not serious. As I often say at workshops and over the air, "Never commit to those who won't commit."

Sending Double Messages: If You Can't Fight 'Em, Join 'Em

Delores and Naomi are obviously sending out mixed signals: broadcasting sexual availability while using sex to gain love. They remind me of a former client who once called my telephone answering service from an airport while she was waiting to change planes on her way home from a weekend in Los Angeles. The service contacted me to answer an emergency call, so I dialed her cell phone number right away.

Catherine had flown to the West Coast for what she had described to me as a "getaway weekend fling" with a superstar basketball player. When she arrived, he parked her in his apartment, then took off to a party and other events "you wouldn't like." Throughout the entire weekend, they only got together around 4 A.M, when he finally got home to his bed.

All they shared was bodily fluids. No, they didn't practice safe sex either, and that's another problem!

Catherine sobbed as she said she knew he was hiding her from all his local women. His shabby treatment made her realize that even though she'd acted as if all she wanted were a few days of hot sex, she really desired much more. She'd never felt so much pain and shame from rejection in all her life.

As I listened to Catherine sob out her story, I wondered if this young generation of black people hasn't been bombarded by too much awareness that few things in this life last. Fashions don't last; products don't last. Young people see love come and then go, as parents, friends, and family marry and divorce over and over. Even life is short, as so many of their peers are violated and lost to prison and death. Convinced that love is an impossible dream anyway, they never stop to consider what all this casual sex and pretense does to their self-esteem.

A major component in adult loving is the ability to integrate tenderness with sexuality, which means you are able to make love to the person for whom you care. Love is not tenderness *or* sex. Love is both. You are able to experience both sexual desire and feelings of care toward your partner. Men and women who do not reach this mature level of integrating emotional attachment and sex find that sexuality becomes their only means of validating themselves and their worth. They may want love desperately, but they are so needy of attention that they send out signals to broadcast their availability for short-term sex. That behavior leads to a vicious cycle of rejection, shame, self-doubt, and a developing sense of being unlovable, which then sparks off an even stronger need for attention. The longer the woman acts out this pattern on the social scene, the more rejections she suffers. She becomes even more desperate for superficial sexual attention, and her attitude grows and grows.

Of course, this is particularly true if a woman has not worked on validating herself in other ways. If she needs men's attention to validate her, when she gets older, she fears the loss of what she's always counted on: the attractiveness that always won attention and was her main calling card for love. Desperation about losing her looks and that validation can lead even a mature woman to present herself as a sexual object, even though she really wants a loving relationship.

I'm amazed by Lillian, a fifty-six-year-old mother of four whom I often bump into at the gym, where we often ride the stationary bikes as she shares her man tales. This civil court judge decks herself out during her off hours in hoochie-mama gear—towering "fuck me" shoes, high-heeled mules that come off with the toss of a foot; tight pants that reveal every crevice, fold, and curve; and a low-cut, stretch T-shirt that hugs her huge bosom.

I've walked out of the gym with her a few times, and we've stopped off at a restaurant to get a bite to eat. Many men will give Lillian a glance or two. But who knows why they look? Her attire is not appropriate for her size, age, and standing in life. It simply does not reflect who she really is.

The last time we shared a meal, she confided her frustration over the types of men she attracts—the street cleaners, the delivery boys, taxi drivers. These are not the men she wants in her life. "I'd never be seen with the likes of them," she huffed indignantly. She doesn't realize that she will never get what she wants until she changes her style so she's sending a different message. Yet Lillian persists in dressing this way because she has to know she hasn't lost it, that she can still turn a man's head.

Another double message many sisters send out involves their own unacknowledged commitment phobia: they *say* they want a committed relationship, but when the right man shows up, they become too afraid to get close, so they settle for sex. Most black women believe that only men behave in this way. They refuse to acknowledge their own fear of connection. Yet many woman have issues about getting close to a man because they've been abandoned and hurt too many times in the past, including by their own fathers.

They may yearn to share their lives with a caring partner, but they are equally terrified of finding that partner, only to be abandoned and rejected yet again.

While I was sitting in the beauty salon the other day, I overheard a conversation between three friends: Lorraine, Shirley, and Dorothea.

Lorraine had recently met a man while she was jogging. They took the same path every morning, and on this particular day, they both stopped to stretch in the same place, at the same time. They began talking, and it turned out that he was divorced and not dating anyone. They agreed to get together. Lorraine said she liked that he was into health, taking care of his body, and seemed to be pleasant. They began dating, but the next thing Lorraine knew, she was discovering all these irritating habits. She didn't like the way he slurped his coffee, the way he always seemed to be clearing his throat before he kissed her, and he seemed to drive his car a little too slowly and cautiously.

"Girls, let me tell you," she told her two friends, "all of them are alike. They look good until you spend time with them and discover they ain't got much going on."

"Are you still seeing him?" Dorothea asked.

"Girl, he got on my last nerve. I had to let him go."

"That doesn't make any sense," Shirley interjected. "Couldn't you have just worked with him a little bit more?"

"Oh, girl, shut up," Dorothea said. "You didn't last so long with Don, and you both go to the same church every Sunday!"

"Well, you know, I liked Don," Shirley said. "He was too quiet though, and he dressed too old-time. Plus, he wasn't into dancing and going to concerts, and he was a little conservative in bed. I found him boring."

"It's terrible when you get old and cynical," observed Dorothea. "Y'all are as picky as you can be. I met me a fine man at Macy's the other day. I was in the men's department looking for a shirt for Father's Day for my brother, and the next thing I knew, my elbow hit the most wonderful elbow. I said, 'Excuse me,' and he smiled. He offered to help me pick out a sweater for my brother, and we started talking. He's a nice guy, a truck driver, lives in the area, and has been single for a long, long time. I think I'm going to pursue it, even though we're only talking on the phone right now, and I'm still figuring out where he's coming from. I don't want to make any mistakes like you girls."

Actually, their mistakes were not their choices of men. The way these women got themselves into trouble was by failing to understand that fear of being hurt again compelled them to look for excuses to get out of these situations before they got in too deep. This is the classic commitment-phobic pattern:

move two steps forward, then four steps back. This little dance is always followed by whining and crying about the loving relationship that they wish they had. These women sincerely want to meet the right man, but they desire just as fervently not to make any more mistakes and create any more suffering for themselves. They want a relationship, but they don't want their lives to become too complicated with issues, and most of all, they fear that another rejection or betrayal would be the end of them. So they construct a lengthy list of requirements that cover everything from complexion shade to height to style of dress—all relatively meaningless factors that work for them by making a relationship even more difficult to achieve.

All this pickiness creates a terrible sense of frustration because it leads to a double bind: you're stuck between wanting something so much and being deathly afraid of it. Many commitment phobes fill their lives with a great deal of activity, including working long hours, so no time or energy is left for a relationship. Of course, they can't see their way out of the vicious cycle of frustration, disappointment, and depression they've created.

One woman I know desperately wants to get married. She was married and divorced early in life and has been dating a man who's been legally separated from his wife for eight years. He keeps assuring her that he will get a divorce, but he never does. She continues in the relationship, protesting all the while that she wants very much to take it to the next level. Deep down, below the surface of her conscious awareness, she's afraid of a second failed marriage. She knows he's never going to get that divorce, so she sticks with him because he's "safe."

A Natural Woman without Guilt

Women who work on boosting their self-esteem often become more self-accepting, confident, and less conflicted about sex as they grow older. Angel is a forty-six-year-old corporate administrator living in Ohio, who tells me that she's been through "many changes" since her college years. Back then, she was sexually intimidated, nonorgasmic, and embarrassed about her large breasts and big butt.

After years of soul-searching and psychotherapy, Angel developed higher self-esteem and began feeling more comfortable with herself as an empowered woman. In fact, Angel feels so liberated today that she often finds herself advising younger women on how to free themselves from anxiety and guilt so they can enjoy sex more.

"You gotta be your own freak," she says. "Nice girls who wait for someone to come to them become frustrated. I feel no frustration. I am totally in control of what I want to do. I take full responsibility for what I need and do. If I don't get what I want, it's on me. I've had great relationships, and I have had great sex. This is my motto: 'I did it and I'm glad. No regrets.'

"I've had a good friend in another state for the past twenty years who is 'my blast from the past,' I go back to him every couple of months for repeat performances. Sometimes you have to accept that you've found a wonderful friend and sex partner, but it just isn't going to work out the way you'd like. So whenever we get together, it's wonderful, just as long as I'm free to do what I need to do. I don't expect men to be responsible for my sexual needs. Women need to understand that sex is a gift, but they have to be selective, take control, and give themselves permission to enjoy that pleasure.

"If you want sex, you gotta be willing to start the show. Give him the signs and don't be afraid of rejection. Rejection doesn't feel as bad as not being around a man at all. I know that the way I look and the way I present myself stirs up a lot of passion in men. I have developed a cocky sense of confidence over the years about my attractiveness, and I flaunt it. I'm not ashamed."

First and foremost, become comfortable with your sexuality before you try to feel that way with anyone else, Angel advises. She believes in what she calls her "penis power." She takes full control in any setting that includes a man she wants to know. She will stake out her claim, find a way to maneuver closer, then invoke her skills at starting an interesting conversation. She flirts but never lets him know her ultimate plan. She'll move away at some point and chat with other people. If she notices that he can't take his eyes off her, she knows she's got his interest. She plays him like a fish on a line.

"That's all well and good," I said after Angel had laid out her entire strategy. "But what's a lady to do if she doesn't like to meet men at clubs and parties, and she feels guilty about having sex without romance?"

"Well, it just means you have to get into household gadgets." I was a little confused about where she was headed. "You know, the gadgets you get in Kmart or the drugstore."

"Are you talking about gadgets that are battery-operated and have a lot of power? The kind of things you would pick up at the Pleasure Chest sex store?"

"Oh, no," she said. "Some women won't go to the Pleasure

Chest, but they will buy something for therapeutic massage at a drugstore. I learned a long time ago that if I couldn't enjoy sexual pleasure with myself, I couldn't have sex without guilt with a man."

After talking with Angel, I realized that she had been through many changes with the men in her life and she'd accepted some home truths about how to take care of herself.

Guilt-free women like Angel don't operate according to anyone else's principles. They've taken the time to sort out their feelings about where they've been, what they've put up with, and they've rethought all those old messages in their head about the do's and don'ts of sex. Then, they go ahead and establish their own moral codes. They understand that it's really up to them to determine what works best for their needs. They've gone within to discover their personal truths and the courage to live according to their own rules, even if some people never accept their choices.

These women know that they can't live for other people. Trying to please others at the expense of your true self is always a setup for the intense level of misery that creates bad attitudes.

Sex Insurance: R.E.S.P.E.C.T.

Not matter how confident and free a sexually active woman may be, she still has to take responsibility for her behavior and the possible repercussions. Good judgment will keep your pride and dignity intact. Sometimes, after the man's long gone, that's all you've got left. Take time out right now to think about a list you can develop of what you need to preserve your sex R.E.S.P.E.C.T. Here are some examples of what I'm talking about:

- Don't run around randomly advertising what you do with the men in your life. Gossip hurts. Remember the double standard still rules.

- Don't date other women's men. This will result in embarrassment for you and hurt for the other woman. It's hard to live with that fallout.

- Try not to tease, provoke, or lead a man on when you have no intention of becoming sexual with him.

- Don't leave yourself vulnerable to disease by going on a date without your supplies: condoms and other birth control.

- Don't create embarrassing public scenes over a man who is not committed to you.

- Don't sleep with his friends. It's not fair, but word will get around that you are cheap and loose.

Now add any other points you think will allow you to enjoy yourself while maintaining sexual R.E.S.P.E.C.T.

Ladies, it's time to own your stuff, to figure out what it is you really want in the bedroom. Escape your prison of frustration, guilt, and shame. If you don't want to settle down right now, that's okay. But if you do want to settle down, don't send double messages to ease the pain of your sexual conflicts. That just complicates life. It is time to own your own stuff. Take the time to figure out what is truly best for your sexual life, which means being in touch with your feelings. Use your personal principles to guide you toward good judgments. Be your own person. Indulge in sex, or take time out from sex if you need the space to learn more about yourself so you can grow. Remember: You can't feel good about sex if you don't feel good about yourself.

Reframe your
thoughts from
negative to positive
by changing your
inner dialogue.

Six

Taking Responsibility

A woman's bad attitude, whatever style it takes, always represents how she projects responsibility for her romantic failures onto everyone but herself, especially onto any man who doesn't come through for her. In other words, a bad attitude represents the way in which a woman plays her blame game.

No matter what your attitude—rage, control, desperation, materialism, mothering, shame, or cynicism—if you want to change your luck in love, you must peel away that protective armor so you can begin to recognize the choices that keep getting you into trouble so that you can begin taking responsibility for your life.

Arnella wanted me to help her make her boyfriend commit to her and to break her addiction to Internet romances. During the past year, the thirty-six-year-old receptionist had spent endless hours on the Internet, hunting for a mate in various chat rooms. "It's easy to be sexy and provocative when you're just typing out words," she confided. "When you're actually face-to-face, all the inhibitions kick in."

Duane was her most recent Internet conquest, but Arnella was distraught because things hadn't worked out as planned. From the very beginning, she'd made it clear that she was looking for a relationship, not a booty call, and Duane vowed that he wanted the same.

"He acted like I was just what he'd been waiting for," she told me. "I know I gave him everything he wanted from a woman. I cooked for him, bought him expensive gifts, and the sex was to die for—so hot and passionate that I wanted it all of the time. But Duane was always moving. He never wanted to spend the night. He'd jump up after sex, wash off real fast, grab his clothes, and head out the door.

"Then I noticed that he only called me from work or his cell phone. When I asked about it, he said his job kept him on the move. And when I asked why we couldn't spend more time together, he pulled this long, sad face and said there was something he had to share."

"Arnella, you're what I've been looking for all my life," Duane had told her, then he spun his tale of woe about a suicidal wife he couldn't leave just yet. He asked Arnella to be patient until he could get his wife to move out.

Arnella was angry that Duane hadn't told her up front that he was married, but he seemed so genuinely unhappy that she felt sorry for him. She believed he really wanted her and would leave his wife as soon as he could. She couldn't abandon him now. Plus, she was too hooked, emotionally and physically.

Shortly after this heart-to-heart, though, they began spending more time chatting on-line and less time together in person. Whenever Duane did come by, it was after a fight with the wife, and he'd spend the time complaining bitterly about feeling stuck. Arnella consoled him with his favorite meals and cute little gifts, and she always made sure to look hot, so he would realize what he was missing.

After several months went by with no change, Arnella began calling his office and paging him, but he never seemed happy to hear from her. Finally, she demanded a showdown: if he didn't come over, she would go to his home and talk to his wife. Duane was shocked: he had never given Arnella his home address or phone number.

When he arrived at her house that night, Arnella was ready—bathed, perfumed, and posing in her sexiest lingerie. Duane told her how sorry he was that they couldn't spend much time together anymore, and he vowed to change his ways. They ended up in bed making wild, passionate love.

The very next day, Duane pulled back even further, until he began refusing her calls and ignoring her pages altogether. Furious, Arnella threatened again to put her "payback program" into effect. Duane was terrified and rushed over again to beg Arnella's forgiveness. He'd never meant to lead her on, he said, but his wife was pregnant, and they'd decided to seek counseling to save their marriage. It was the only right thing to do. Couldn't he and Arnella just be friends?

She flew into a rage. "I have enough friends!" she screamed. "What I want is a husband and the family that you promised me!" Duane had never promised a family, and when he pointed that out, Arnella became even more crazed. After he left, she tore her apartment apart, then cried herself to sleep.

Despite her time and trouble, nothing had worked. Arnella had run out of options, so she wound up in my office, feeling angry and depressed.

Arnella's story is familiar. From the very first night, she had ample evidence that Duane was a poor prospect for anything long-term. But she ignored the obvious signs and went with her emotions fueled by fantasies that commanded her to "find a man at any cost."

Of course, while she was obsessing over having Duane and only Duane, Arnella was ignoring other men who might have been better candidates for the long term. Women like Arnella could save themselves a lot of heartache if they would only pick up on the clues right under their noses.

Don't Be a Blame Jane

Answer the following questions with a *yes* or *no*. They will help you check yourself so you can begin withdrawing your blame from others and taking ownership of your decisions:

1. Do you usually blame others for any of your difficult situations?
    Yes_____ No_____

2. Do you use anger or rage to force others to take on the blame or guilt?
    Yes_____ No_____

3. Do you think of yourself as powerless or helpless?
    Yes_____ No_____

4. Do you lack faith in yourself to make the right decisions?

   Yes_____ No_____

5. Do you repeat the same negative relationship pattern without searching for its root in your own emotional issues?

   Yes_____ No_____

6. Do you constantly ask the same question: "Why is this happening to me?"

   Yes_____ No_____

7. Do you feel the world and all the men in it are against you?

   Yes_____ No_____

Taking Responsibility for Your Choices

Arnella couldn't establish a healthy love relationship because her attitudes of rage and shame drove her to make rash, poorly thought-out decisions that got her the wrong results. These included looking for a mate over the Internet and blindly accepting as gospel everything Duane told her. Arnella's real problem wasn't that she was single, but that she believed things just "happened" to her. She was unable to recognize and take responsibility for the choices that led to these troublesome situations.

Arnella wanted me to help her get Duane to leave his pregnant wife. In spite of everything, Arnella was still convinced that she had to have this man. No matter how many times he told her no, she remained consumed with making him come around.

My goal was different. I wanted to encourage Arnella to drop her attitudes of rage and shame by helping her put an end to her blame game. Men like Duane are everywhere, but the choice to be with them or not to be with them rests entirely with the woman. He is who he is, and that's unlikely to change. Therefore, it's up to the woman to keep her eyes open and make decisions about the relationship based on what she observes.

Duane was clearly unavailable for a genuine, monogamous relationship, yet Arnella, and many women like her, will go on and on about all the terrible things men like Duane do to them. Somehow, it never occurs to these women to give up that blame game and start taking responsibility for their misguided choice to hang in there.

If you spend your life blaming someone else for the decisions you make, you are turning over control of your life to someone else. Arnella was in a constant hysterical rage and totally out of control because she persisted in forcing romantic situations that never had a chance, and she blamed those failures on the men.

Letting the Past Rule Your Present

After Arnella had poured out the tale of this latest misadventure in her lengthy saga of disappointing relationships, I began questioning her about her childhood. Attitudes don't result only from romantic disappointments in adulthood. They are usually rooted in patterns of loving that you learned from your family as a child.

Arnella grew up with two sisters and two brothers and both parents, in a nice, middle-class, suburban neighborhood with all the trappings of luxury. But she was a middle child who never felt she received enough love or attention. She adored her father, but he spent most of his time working away from home. Now that she was looking back on her childhood, she told me, she realized that her mother seemed depressed all the time, probably about her unsatisfying marriage. With her husband out somewhere all the time, Arnella's mother was forced to cope with four kids by herself. Arnella remembered a constant sense that something was missing and thinking to herself, "The day I finish school and get out of this family, I'm going to get a job and make my own family with a husband who will be there for me."

When Arnella reached her senior year of college, she set out to look for that husband, just as she had promised herself. She dated, but none of the relationships lasted beyond three months. During her last semester of college, a familiar longing returned to haunt her. Arnella visited the school counselor, but he told her not to worry. Depression was typical of girls her age. She just needed time to get over it.

Arnella graduated and began teaching in a Long Island, New York, school system. Soon, she noticed that whenever she didn't have a date for the weekend, and sometimes even during the week, she'd stop by the deli before she got on the train and buy a nice apple strudel. It would be gone before she reached her stop. On her way home from the station, she'd stop at the Häagen-Dazs ice-cream store. At home, she'd fry up a hamburger, but after she'd eat it, she was usually still hungry, so she'd prepare one, maybe two, more. As she settled in for an evening in front of the TV, she'd start in on the ice cream and wind up polishing off the entire container. Before she turned off the lights, she'd go back into the kitchen to get bags of potato chips, popcorn, and cookies so they'd be ready on the bedside table, in case she got hungry during the night. Arnella was often surprised to wake up the next morning in a sea of crumbs.

After the first few months of eating this way, Arnella was horrified to discover that she'd gained thirty pounds. She immediately went on a starvation diet until she shed the weight. That launched a pattern of gaining weight as loneliness overwhelmed her, then starving it off. Of course, when she was overweight, she felt even worse about herself and more reluctant to go out anywhere she could meet men. So she developed bulimia, which allowed her to eat as much as she wanted, then regurgitate the food. Arnella didn't even know that this eating disorder is called bulimia. In fact, when she came to see me, she didn't even realize she had an eating disorder that needed to be treated. Obviously, Arnella was filling the emotional void in her life with food, especially comfort foods. Instead of eating, she needed to discover what was eating her.

I was able to help Arnella connect her past longing for a loving and nurturing father figure with her present acting out of that longing through overeating and hooking up with unavailable men. As an adult, she was setting up scenarios with men that paralleled both her own childhood rejection from her father and the dynamic she had observed playing out between her parents. In other words, she was choosing men who were as reluctant to connect as her father, then trying to make them love her, just as she had struggled to win Daddy's love.

One day in the midst of our discussion of her eating problem, Arnella was shocked by a sudden recollection of her childhood disgust at her mother's obesity. Her mother must also have coped with her loneliness by filling the emptiness with food!

For Arnella to overcome her depression, her eating disorder, and her overwhelming need for connection with a man, she had to learn how to identify, express, and accept her feelings. In particular, Arnella had to work through the deep-seated pain associated with the original loss of her father's love. Finally, Arnella had to reframe her self-image so she'd lose the belief that she was fundamentally unlovable and that Daddy hadn't spent time with her or loved her enough because she wasn't worthy of his time and love.

Hanging On to Losing Situations

After years of frustration over not finding a man of their own, women like Arnella often decide to "make themselves a man." They meet a brother whose shortcomings are woefully obvious, but they ignore the evidence right under their noses and "work with him" anyway, because he's all they have at the moment. They mistakenly believe that if they put more and more effort into a losing situation, ultimately it will turn around, and they'll finally get the outcome they want.

When the relationship fails despite all their efforts to force it, these women go ballistic. They're furious at the man for not living up to their expectations—and by extension, they're angry at the entire world. This failure is yet another loss on top of too many others. Now that another investment hasn't paid off, all they can see before them is an endless mateless future.

The problem is that these women don't realize that each romantic failure reopens and exacerbates that old wound of childhood abandonment and sets them up for the next unhappy relationship.

At the same time, the prospect of real love—a condition they've never experienced—is terrifying. Of course, these women are totally unaware of their fear that if they ever were to find true love, they would surely lose him. The pain of that loss would be absolutely unbearable. So while they talk often and loudly about how much they crave a genuine, lasting relationship with a "real man," they are, in fact, scared to death of that profound level of intimacy and the risks it would entail.

Fear of intimacy is the real reason why women choose men who are even more unwilling to commit than themselves. These women act out their own fears of intimacy by becoming involved with unavailable men to avoid the greatest threat of all: connecting with a man with whom they could have a satisfying relationship only to lose him. They forge blindly ahead, trying over and over to make themselves a man, then suffering each time a doomed attempt fails to work out. These women "forget" the old axiom: *When you get involved with someone who is already involved with someone else, you get the leftovers, never the main course.* They don't understand what they're really doing or why they're doing it, because somewhere deep inside they believe that all they deserve are leftovers.

Are You like Arnella?

Arnella could have avoided all that rage, desperation, and despair if she had been willing to give up her soap opera fantasies and take responsibility for her choices.

Are you like Arnella, disappointed in love because you are controlled by attitudes that keep you tied to fantasies and unable to accept reality? Find out by answering the following questions with a *yes* or *no*.

1. Do you allow your emotions to take over your thinking and your life?
   Yes_____ No_____

2. Do you frequently decide you must have something or someone no matter what the actual circumstances?
   Yes_____ No_____

3. Do you vacillate between blaming yourself and the man because the relationship is failing?
   Yes_____ No_____

4. Do you have trouble telling the difference between your "wants" and your "needs?"
   Yes_____ No_____

5. Do you focus your entire life on what you believe is missing from it, rather than working with the possibilities that are present?
Yes_____ No_____

6. Do you become enraged with a man if he fails to live up to your expectations?
Yes_____ No_____

7. Do you feel you have no influence over what takes place in your relationships?
Yes_____ No_____

8. Do you believe you can change a man into the one you need him to be?
Yes_____ No_____

9. Do you believe that you must have sex with a particular man in order to feel okay?
Yes_____ No_____

Even if you answered yes to only one of the questions, you need to read on.

Are You a Drama Queen?

Arnella is clearly a drama queen who fuels her belief that her relationship with Duane was based on love by making sure to surround it with a lot of emotion. Do you confuse "being in love" with your emotional intensity?

Here is a quiz that will help you figure out if your own

emotions are running at fever pitch, overwhelming your life and everyone else around you.

Taking Your Emotional Temperature

Answer the following questions with *yes, no,* or *sometimes:*

1. Are most of your relationships with men unstable, chaotic, or intense?
   Yes_____ No_____ Sometimes_____

2. Do you suffer from extreme mood shifts that tend to last a few hours or days at a time?
   Yes_____ No_____ Sometimes_____

3. Do you ever experience intense, uncontrollable anger that is inappropriate to a situation?
   Yes_____ No_____ Sometimes_____

4. Do you abuse food, alcohol, or drugs?
   Yes_____ No_____ Sometimes_____

5. Do you ever feel empty and bored?
   Yes_____ No_____ Sometimes_____

6. Do you ever feel anxious, restless, or have difficulty focusing?
   Yes_____ No_____ Sometimes_____

7. Do you become extremely annoyed if you have to wait for service in a line, drive behind a slow driver, or are put on hold by an operator?
   Yes_____ No_____ Sometimes_____

8. Do you become annoyed whenever you're asked to perform a simple favor, and do you allow that reaction to show?

   Yes_____ No_____ Sometimes_____

9. Do you act out your anger by slamming doors, throwing things, withdrawing your attention, sulking, and/or threatening to abandon a person or situation forever?

   Yes_____ No_____ Sometimes_____

10. When you are angry, do you call out someone's name in the nastiest, loudest, most degrading way possible?

    Yes_____ No_____ Sometimes_____

11. Do you ever lose control of yourself to such an extent that you try to do bodily damage to the object of your rage by throwing something at him or even striking him?

    Yes_____ No_____ Sometimes_____

Rage is probably the attitude sisters most display. If you have an attitude of rage, it could be the root of your problems with relationships. It's important to determine whether you display rage, especially since brothers automatically run for cover whenever a women goes on the attack. You may be carrying anger over unfinished childhood business—perhaps sexual, physical, or verbal abuse—and it's been compounded by your frustrations in adult relationships. In any case, all that rage has been stored up inside for years. As it struggles to express itself, the pressure keeps building, so you release it bit by bit, on all the wrong people.

Perhaps you felt unloved or abandoned by a parent because of divorce or other circumstances. You may be acting out childhood rage over being left behind, neglected, or unloved in each new relationship, because each new man is, after all, another "potential abandoner."

The powerlessness you may have experienced as a child when you were immersed in family craziness probably allowed no space for expressing your feelings and trying to heal your pain. As an adult, you still don't know how to heal your pain, so you try instead to control others with the whip of your anger and lots of drama.

Beverly's Story

Beverly, a heavyset, forty-year-old hospital administrator who'd never been married, came to see me because after all this time, she had finally met a man. Suddenly, though, she found herself too afraid to settle in with him. He was living with her, but she refused to get married, and she was plagued with serious doubts about the relationship.

Larry was a recovering alcoholic, but he had a full-time job and was even helping Beverly around the house. Even more important, his behavior suggested that he truly loved and cared for her.

Yet Beverly was upset when she walked into my office. She wanted to know right away what she should do about this man: Should she let him remain in her home or put him out?

I decided to probe a little further to discover why Beverly was so anxious to get rid of Larry when she was also telling me that she'd spent all her life looking for a relationship and that this man was actually coming through for her. He was showing her love without seeming to want more than her love in return. What was making her so uncomfortable? I suspected that Beverly was blinded by attitudes of control and mothering. She seemed afraid to let go and leave herself vulnerable, especially since Larry was offering a type of relationship she had never experienced. She just couldn't trust it.

I suspected that Beverly was stuck on the belief that since she couldn't depend on anyone, it was better for others to need her. Larry only needed her love, so she felt threatened in some powerful but inexplicable way.

I asked Beverly to tell me about her childhood. I was shocked by the story that unfolded.

When Beverly was ten months old, her mother left Beverly's father and moved to New York to pursue a career in entertainment. Beverly was handed over to her father's mother. Two years later, Beverly's mother gave birth to a son, whom she kept with her, but Beverly only heard from her mother by telephone or through other relatives.

"Why wasn't I chosen to be the one who lived with Mama?" she remembers wondering. As she looked back, Beverly said she was just beginning to realize that her mother's abandonment was the first major disappointment of her life, a traumatic event.

Her father was in the military and away a lot, but he did visit and send his mother money to pay for Beverly's care. Whenever her father was home on furlough, he'd stay with his mother. Beverly was always jumping in his lap and begging for his attention. She thought he was the most wonderful person in the world.

I asked Beverly to tell me about her other family relationships.

"Well, I think I have to tell you more about this one," she said. "Something really serious happened to me, but I don't know how deep you want me to get here."

"As deep as you want to go," I replied.

"Well, at about the age of ten, I was sexually abused by my father," she told me almost matter-of-factly. "He began fondling me."

"Did he tell you to fondle him or did he fondle you?"

"Both. He basically did everything."

"How did all this happen?"

"He would come into my room at night when he was staying with my grandmother, his mother. I was afraid, so I told no one. My father said at one point that I was helping him, and I was always so in awe of my father that I didn't want to do anything that would hurt him. Anyway, I really didn't know what it was that he was doing to me, so I kept letting it happen."

After the father was discharged from the military, he moved in with his mother and the abuse became constant.

"My self-esteem was in serious trouble at this point because I knew what was going on," Beverly told me. "I felt trapped. I didn't know what to do."

At the age of fifteen or sixteen, she couldn't remember exactly when, her father moved into his own place, and she visited him for two weeks during the summer. During that period, her father raped her continually. To this day, she doesn't remember exactly what went on because she remembers going into an out-of-body state every time he approached her for sex.

Beverly returned to her grandmother feeling agitated and unsettled. She couldn't focus on schoolwork, and she began acting up in class and getting into trouble. Ironically, her grandmother's solution was to send Beverly to live with her father permanently. Now, her father could have intercourse with her again and again and again. By now, her half brother was visiting her at her father's place. Many years later, she discovered that he had heard her crying out for help at night, but he never told anyone or tried to help. Beverly even revealed to me that she suspected that her aunt, her father's sister who had moved next door, had an idea of what was going on. But no one protected Beverly.

"No one protected you?" I asked Beverly. This was a key issue.

"No one."

"They kind of left you out there. What a little kid needs at that point in her life is protection."

Beverly continued her story. She managed to finish high school, but she was depressed most of the time and burdened by tremendous issues about her sexuality. If a boy wanted her, was it for her or just for what she could do for him? She was always confused about that. When she was twenty-three, she had her first serious relationship, but it only lasted a year. Then she went through a series of short, doomed relationships.

"I guess I always fall for the wrong type," she commented.

"What do you mean?" I asked. "What are the types you fall for?"

"Street guys. I hate to say it, but they've always been the ne'er-do-wells."

"What do you mean?"

"They usually need to be rescued and supported financially. Almost always they're down on their luck, jobless, homeless, and looking for love."

"What do you usually do?"

"I usually help them find work. I give them money. I even give them emotional support. I become their therapist."

I asked if she ever found them apartments or bought them clothes.

"Normally, I let them shack up with me," she said with a tight little smile. "I got a reputation for doing that."

Attitudes and the Inner Child

During early development, every child needs protection, love, guidance, and the comforting sense that he or she is cared for. When children don't receive this emotional nurturing, they doubt their ability to be loved, and that has a powerfully negative effect on their self-esteem. They are left with big questions concerning the possibility of anyone ever wanting and loving them. Like Beverly, these children eventually spend their entire adult lives reliving that abandonment scenario, over and over, in each relationship.

The healthy part of Beverly wanted real love, but the unhealthy part of her, the part that had "accepted" she was unworthy of love, made sure she wouldn't get it by repeatedly becoming involved with the wrong men. These conflicting desires—to be loved and to avoid love—are always present at the same time. In Beverly's case, she had learned that she had to "take care" of her father to keep his love, so as an adult, Beverly overcompensated whenever a man came into her life. Her insecurities led her to overrescue, overprotect, overgive, and over-identify with these men's neediness so they would love her and she would not have to re-experience the pain and shame she knew all too well. At the same time, her healthy aspect understood that these men were totally incapable of real love.

My job was to help Beverly recognize this pattern that ran from her childhood throughout her adult history with men. She needed to realize that her doubts about Larry had more to do with her fears about taking a risk with a man who was available and not overly needy than with any of his actual shortcomings, real or imagined. When she'd first become involved with Larry, he seemed, on the surface, to conform to her usual pattern. But Larry was not irrevocably damaged. He had beaten his alcoholism and was learning to take responsibility for his choices. He was open and ready to love her, and Beverly was now confronted with the challenge of working through her fears of inadequacy.

Confronting Anger, Pain, and Fear

I suggested to Beverly that she was trying to clean up her past by identifying with men who were helpless, hopeless, and needed protection and rescuing, just as she had when she was a little girl being abused by her father. She understood their need for care and protection so well that she had projected the pain of her own neediness onto these men. Of course, it worked out beautifully for them since they were dependent types anyway.

Beverly's discomfort with Larry resulted from her deep and unconscious belief that she wasn't entitled to care and nurturing. In spite of what Beverly knows intellectually about childhood abuse, some unconscious part of her still carried the blame for what had happened with her father.

The victim often blames herself for being victimized. Blame, including the guilt of self-blame, always leads to resentment, and if that resentment simmers inside long enough, it can lead to extreme anger, even rage. Along with her attitudes of control and nurturing, Beverly was definitely displaying rage. But until she examined the roots of her attitudes, she would remain stuck in her pattern of controlling, rescuing men and becoming disappointed and angry. She would also continue to reject men like Larry who were willing to commit to a long-lasting, equitable relationship.

"You are more invested in pleasing other people, and living up to their expectations so you'll win their approval, than you are in taking care of yourself," I told Beverly. "Because you feel guilty about your relationship with your father, you've decided that your needs have to come last, that your needs shouldn't matter as much as others'. Your father taught you that by forcing you to meet his needs instead of taking care of yours. You want so much to be accepted because your mother rejected you and your father abused you. What he did suggested that he wanted you, but the price for having your father was 'taking care of him' sexually, which was unnatural and repugnant. Now you're trapped in a self-victimizing cycle where you keep acting out the same situation of taking care of your father with different men. Your self-esteem is extremely damaged, so you don't feel you deserve for anyone to really love you for yourself. Neither the blame nor the shame empowers you. You need to get in touch with your anger so you can then release the feelings that you've been carrying around for so long."

I suggested that Beverly write an "anger letter" to her father. Whether she mailed it was not as important as getting her feelings out. We agreed that in the coming weeks we would work together on the letter and on other ways to vent her emotions about her childhood. Because of her conflicting feelings toward her father, we decided she would address him not as "Father," but by his first name. This is the letter Beverly wrote—and sent:

> Hal,
> It's been years since we've been in touch with each other. Now, you're in your later years and I am approaching my middle years as an adult. I've been through a lot in my life and I've done a lot of soul-searching. I've also sought professional guidance so I can deal with the unfinished business between you and me. I've come to the conclusion that though I never want to see you again, I need to put a closure on all this. So I've decided to write to you in order to let you know how I feel so I can finally heal.
> Have you ever, just once, in all your life, realized how

much you have damaged mine? I cannot conceive in my own mind how a father could rape his own daughter, then tell her over and over again, in order to confuse this child, that she is helping him? You took advantage of my natural need for your acceptance and love. How could you? As a little girl, I didn't realize how sick you are and how perverted your behavior was. Because of you, I have felt like dirt, unworthy of real love. All my life I've hidden from men by being obese, because I felt so ashamed, and I was in so much pain from never being loved by you. Even when I tried to enjoy making love, I couldn't because I felt so guilty and dirty. It's only now, after so many years and working hard in psychotherapy, that I am finally ready to have a healthy relationship with a man.

You're probably wondering why it took so many years for me to address this. Well, it's taken many years for me, one, to feel that I'm a valuable person and, two, to accept love. Three, I'm finally ready for what life has to offer me. The most important thing I realize at this stage of my life is that nothing you did to me was my fault. It was all yours. Now you live with it.

Good-bye

"Anger letters," "grief letters," and "forgiveness letters" can be effective means of releasing a piece of your history that is blocking your opportunities for happiness and fulfillment.

You can use Beverly's letter to her father as a model for your own letter to a troublesome figure from your past. Writing a letter is a good beginning step toward expressing and releasing buried emotions and unproductive behavior patterns that stem from your childhood. These old emotions and issues create the attitudes that keep you stuck in worn-out behavior patterns and prevent you from finding love today.

Emotional Baggage

All of us have issues left over from our past, especially from childhood. The important point is to stop denying those issues and the emotions and behaviors they create. Whatever is denied will rule you because all that energy is struggling to be released and you are constantly fighting back to keep it suppressed. The struggle is futile, because you always wind up acting out these buried issues and emotions anyway within the framework of your present relationships. You may be unaware of this dynamic, but believe me, the only way to jump off the Wheel of Misfortune is by becoming aware of the issues and emotions that are running your life, so you can finally resolve them and be free. Only then can you make conscious and productive choices regarding men, as well as virtually every other aspect of your life.

Some of you may find that you need professional guidance to help you identify and work through issues, emotions, and behaviors that are tied to your past. In that case, I urge you to seek professional counseling. Unfortunately, many of us have a problem with seeking professional counseling because of the common misperception that you have to be "crazy" to receive that type of help.

Know that none of us gets through life without carrying some piece of "baggage" from our childhood, and the best way to travel through life is as lightly—that is, as productively—as possible.

One way to discover what issues you may be carrying around is by identifying your trouble areas in the present.

Make a list of five things that bother you the most about your relationships, your career, and your family:

1.

2.

3.

4.

5.

The next section will guide you to a better understanding of how your trouble areas in the present connect to your experiences in the past. The following questions help you examine your past. Use your answers to see how they link to the above list of your life's trouble areas. This will give you better understanding of how childhood issues may relate to your current problems, especially in your relationships.

Unpacking Emotional Baggage

All of us, to some extent, are products of our past. As I've already stated, no one gets through life without accumulating some emotional damage. The trick is to understand your own issues so that you are no longer compelled to act them out. At the same time, you need to become as aware as possible of the issues a potential romantic partner could be bringing to your relationship. Once you have a good idea of where you are and what you can expect from him, you can respond as constructively as possible to whatever comes up.

The following questions will help you figure out what kind of baggage you are carrying and how heavy your load is. You can also use these questions at another time to help you assess a potential partner's emotional baggage:

1. How extensive was the emotional damage done to you or him when you/he was a child? Here are some categories to help you determine in what way(s) you/he may have been traumatized:

    (a) Sexual abuse and sexual trauma

    (b) Physical or verbal abuse

    (c) Parental abandonment

    (d) Parental addictions (gambling, drugs, alcohol, womanizing, etc.)

    (e) Present-day eating disorders

2. Are you (is he) aware of your/his emotional damage and how it's affected your/his ability to relate to a romantic partner?

3. Are you (is he) working on your/his issues in order to resolve them through therapy, seminars, retreats, friends, church, and other means by which people are counseled?

Some of us are lugging around trunk loads of past trauma; the lucky ones tote carry-on bags. But all of us are weighted down by something. The more we unpack, the more we understand ourselves and the more readily we can adjust our attitudes to create more satisfying patterns of loving.

It's Not Just His Fault

Of course, Duane was a classic drive-by lover, and his behavior was inexcusable. Yet, the real problem was Arnella herself. Desperate, angry women like her must realize that to find love and build a harmonious relationship they first need to resolve a raging struggle within. Arnella's insistence on clinging to her fantasy notions about her relationship with Duane was her way of staying in denial, of avoiding truths about herself and her situation. Many women are consumed by similar inner conflicts. They protect themselves from the truths about themselves with fantasies that distract them from the pain, fear, shame, and frustration that keep welling up.

On the other hand, Beverly knew that Larry was willing and capable of loving her and taking care of her. She just couldn't trust that love. Her ability to trust had been destroyed at a very young age, so she was struggling over her refusal to come to terms with an ingrained but unconscious belief that loving a man would leave her vulnerable and unsafe.

Letting go of your inner struggle is not easy, but it's doable. The biggest step is to recognize and accept those buried feelings so you can spot your patterns of self-defeating behavior. You need to know what drives you.

Arnella's need for control was linked to her need to be right. That is why she never bothered to check whether her fantasy of life with Duane was possible. Arnella's drive to be emotionally connected to a man also brought with it a need to create drama. The drama of their relationship made every-thing seem so emotional, more like her fuzzy notion of what it's like to "be in love." Her drive for security carried with it an intense fear of rejection and loss. Those fears fueled her des-perate attempts to form an attachment.

Beverly was driven by the fear that if she let Larry love her and returned his love, he would eventually reject and betray her. After all, she had loved her father and look what he did! She'd loved her mother, but her mother had left her alone and defenseless and had never returned to save her.

Until women like Arnella and Beverly recognize and acknowledge the feelings and needs that drive them, they will never understand the root of their self-destructive behaviors. Arnella refused to take a good, long look inside herself to understand why she clung to a hopeless situation. She was so fearful of never getting married and having a family that she set out to "make herself a man" instead. When working with that man failed to get her the results she wanted, she projected all the blame for the failure onto Duane because it was too painful to accept responsibility for her own choices. She didn't want to believe that the only way she could have changed the situation was by working on herself. But she needed to confront her fears and, in doing so, defuse their hold over her. Only then would Arnella be able to see the situation with Duane clearly and gain more control over her emotions and behavior.

Fortunately, Beverly was able through therapy to recognize the inner dynamic that was undermining her relationship with Larry. We continue to work together on untangling her present relationship from the web of her past trauma.

Unpacking Your Baggage: Clarity Is Power

For most of us, letting go of the past is an ongoing, lifelong process. The more you unravel from your childhood history, the clearer you become in your present choices. Here are a few suggestions to get you started on putting your past behind you:

• Confront each of your memories of the past and strip away any distortions.

One of the ways to confront your memories is to talk to relatives who might have objective information about your childhood relationships. They can tell you what they observed and what they thought. Sometimes, you discover that things were not as you saw them. Your memories may be distorted. Relatives know what really took place and can clear up past confusion so you can finally let go of the fear and pain.

I once suggested that a male client try to find out from his father's brother why his father had disappeared when the client was a child. He had grown up thinking that his father left because he didn't want a relationship with him. The father was now deceased, so he couldn't be questioned. When my client sat down to talk with his uncle, he learned that all the women on his mother's side had refused to let the father see him. His mother was still alive, so he was able to check out his uncle's story. She hung her head as she admitted, "Yes, we were all so enraged with your father for fooling around with other women that we didn't want any connection. We cut you off from him completely." This new information helped ease the pain my client had been carrying around over his father's apparent rejection.

- Make peace with your childhood situation.

  Know that your parents did the best they could. Your parents were the way they were because of who they are, not because of any faults that lie within you. Once you untangle the past and understand that the circumstances of your childhood weren't your fault, you will be able to see how much you bought into those circumstances and played them out in your adult relationships.

  Untangling your past can be a difficult and lifelong process, but the further along you get toward making peace with your childhood, the better off you are. Don't feel that you have to work through this peacemaking entirely by yourself. Here's where a woman's support group, an older mentor, or even a professional counselor can help you assign the blame of the past to your past.

  Examining your past will help you pinpoint the unfulfilled needs that you are acting out within present relationships.

- Identify your needs.

  The following simple exercise will speed your progress to knowing your needs:

  Identify to the best of your ability your unfulfilled need or needs. Set them down in writing, using as few words as possible and writing in bold lettering on a four-by-six-inch card. For example, you could be like Arnella in your need for unconditional acceptance, love, and support. If so, you would write on the card: "I need to be accepted and loved unconditionally and to be supported absolutely." Or like Beverly, you might need a relationship that is stable and secure. So you would write on the card: "I need a relationship that is stable and secure." If you have more than one need, write each one on a separate index card. Then copy each statement of a need onto two or three more cards. Place one set of cards that describes all of your needs on your night table. Another set of cards can go next to your coffeemaker, or anywhere else you are sure to spot them first thing in the morning. Another set of cards can be in a drawer of your office desk or, if privacy is an issue, in the purse you take to work. You can also leave a set anywhere else you spend regular time, such as the glove compartment of your car.

Review these cards a few times a day and evaluate what actions you are taking to fulfill those needs. If you keep forgetting to read the cards, keep losing them, are too busy to read them, or have to force yourself to read them, you are still stuck in wanting others to take care of these needs for you. Instead of taking responsibility for addressing these needs yourself, you are probably acting them out in your present relationships.

An attitude-free woman accepts being

- vulnerable where she used to be in control
- tender with her feelings rather than sulking in hurt ones
- trusting where she used to be desperate
- compassionate where she used to be angry and harsh
- responsive where she used to be smothering
- realistic where she used to be shameful of social status
- hopeful where she used to be cynical
- self-fulfilling where she used to be materialistic

Flow into the essence
of your true being
and connect with
your true needs.

Seven

The Right Attitude

Hostility Breeds Short-Term Relationships

Angry black women are everywhere you turn. They are the shrill women you don't want to wait on you in a store because you can spot their bad attitudes a mile away. They are the sullen young women you see in malls, often dragging a toddler by the arm. More significantly, too many sisters believe that their hostile feelings toward black men are legitimate. They're convinced that they have good reason to walk around angry—at their men and the world at large.

What is the anger about? They say it's about men not giving them the love they want, but all that anger disconnects people even further. So the black woman's anger over her failure to connect is also the biggest obstacle she confronts in her efforts to make a healthy, happy love connection. How can you get out of this mess? By increasing your ability to deal with frustration and unhappiness. This reduces your need to manipulate everything around you. Once you feel confident and empowered, you don't need to manipulate anyone. Empowerment means that you know you can take care of yourself without the protection of an attitude or trying to change anyone else.

Building Up Your Tolerance for Frustration and Unhappy Feelings

Frustration is a natural part of life. No one is happy all the time, and no one always gets what he or she wants, whenever he or she wants it. Blue days will come. To take control over life, you have to learn to ride out these lows and not come unraveled every time disappointment or misfortune comes your way. Lashing out at others just because you're unhappy never works. We need to learn healthy ways to displace unhappiness and find the faith that better days will come.

Fighting for Control Keeps You out of Control

As I've noted, many women deal with their frustration and the fear that nothing will ever be right in their life by trying to control everything around them. Their constant anxiety keeps them feeling totally helpless and out of control, so they do everything they can to meet their emotional needs by dominating situations and people.

When you try to control everything and everyone around you, a strange thing happens: you lose more control over yourself. Every time I inform my clients of this simple fact—that if you need that much to be in control, you are really out of control—they are shocked. They are so convinced that more control is the only way to calm that inner sense of helplessness. In fact, they often refuse to acknowledge that they are controlling at all. I remember a client who explained that she was merely keeping her life in order and manageable. So whenever her man refused to go along with her program, she became totally outraged and shocked. Women like her believe in keeping on top of their man situation, which means keeping up with his every move and thought. What a high price to pay just to have someone in your life!

Drama Won't Get You Love

Remember Arnella? She convinced herself that she was in love by constantly pushing Duane into loud, emotionally fraught arguments. All that intensity—the yelling, slamming doors, loud threats, throwing things, tears, and the sizzling lovemaking that sometimes followed the battles—gave her a sense that this relationship was "important" and "meaningful," because she was "fighting" for it.

In reality, Arnella was just a drama queen, struggling to be in control and substituting her fantasies about the relationship for the much less exciting reality that she was just Duane's outside stuff. She was living out past trauma in the present, responding not to the realities around her, but to emotional triggers that set off her childhood pain. For Duane, Arnella was little more than a safety valve that allowed him to release pent-up emotions over his real issues in his real relationship with his wife.

How to Cool Down Drama

A "control drama" is a scene or encounter between two people in which one is trying by any means necessary to gain the upper hand. Here are the steps you can take to avoid heated encounters or to cool down a drama that's already on:

1. Check out the details of the drama. Who usually starts it? What situations generally prompt the conflict? How does the script usually play out?

2. Examine how your partner pulls you into the conflict or how you pull him in, and check what each of you do once you are involved.

3. Try walking away . . . nicely. Don't start a drama, and refuse to join in if he wants one. Tell him calmly that you want to discuss the situation, but first, you need to calm down.

4. Don't try to control the other person's behavior. Deal with your own instead.

5. If matters become overheated, be willing to call for time-out and encourage your partner to do the same.

6. Remember that your partner's behavior is not always about you. However, you do need to check whether you have played a role in sparking it off. You may not want to own that fact. Duane was a drive-by lover long before he met Arnella, but her insistence that he fulfill her fantasies caused him to make even more promises that he had no intention of fulfilling.

Dealing with the Here and Now

How can you tell when you are reacting to past experiences instead of responding with clarity and objectivity to current situations?

When you are embroiled in drama, you tend to confuse past issues with what's going on in the immediate situation. The key points listed below will help you separate past issues from present situations so they don't intrude on current possibilities.

- Stop casting blame on others. Taking time to count from one to ten may seem like an old-fashioned tip, but it gives you space to reconsider what's going on. Only you can control your feelings and responses to anyone's actions, including your own. Blaming others doesn't help you resolve your insecurities or ease your pain. Nor will misplacing the blame help you find the way to reclaim your life and your romantic destiny.
- Cultivate awareness of the types of situations you tend to set up so you can play out your victim role. Learn to

identify the cues. One helpful technique is to keep a journal in writing or on audiotape to record the events of your daily life. Review these accounts of your days from time to time. Do you see any patterns emerging? When situations turn sour, ask yourself, what have I done to set them up? What was the emotional payoff for that failed situation? When people disappoint you, ask yourself, what have I done to ensure that they would? What role did I play in that disappointment and how has that disappointment given me what I actually want instead of what I *say* I want?

A model for setting up your journal is given on page 212.

- The stream of negative chatter that runs in your head like a nonstop tape loop is your worst enemy. Become aware of what you are constantly telling yourself. Challenge those beliefs. You will discover that they are completely invalid.
- Identify whatever qualities you need to reinforce in yourself. Higher self-esteem, if you feel unworthy of love; more confidence, if you experience a great deal of anxiety and fear.
- Improve your self-esteem and confidence by venturing into experiences that will challenge your negative beliefs about yourself. Take a course to acquire a skill that interests you. One client who learned how to sail reported to me that the most rewarding part of that experience was not the beauty of the scenery or the physical exercise, but that she'd done it all by herself.

Find an activity that uplifts you and gives your life more meaning. This could be an art or dance class, singing in a choir, or doing volunteer work. Or you could deliberately set out to create a social life for yourself by joining various groups. Remember: You have choices. You can refuse to participate in situations that are not uplifting. You don't have to engage with everyone or every situation that shows up in your life.

- Instead of "self-medicating" your fear, sadness, or anger by overeating or engaging in any other addiction, including sex, accept and express your feelings. Scream if you need to scream; cry if you need to cry. Here's a tip: Screaming into a pillow will muffle the sound so you won't disturb your neighbors. I've had patients who screamed in their cars with the radio turned way up, or in the shower with the water coming down full blast.

- Stop testing other people to affirm that you are acceptable. When you buy someone an expensive gift or take him or her into your home or extend yourself in an extreme way, are you motivated by a hidden agenda? Is that hidden agenda a trade-off—your expectation of a reward? You perform the service and, in return, he or she makes you feel better about yourself? When you place the responsibility of self-acceptance in the hands of others, you give them the right to determine whether you are okay. That never leads to a positive outcome. Other people don't have to be invested in your self-confidence. Only you can make that investment.

How to Set Up Your Journal

The following model for your journal will help you identify and track what situations keep repeating themselves in your day-to-day life and within your relationships. These are the situations that trigger your anger, sadness, frustration, cynicism, or fear, as well as your negative patterns of behavior.

Use a ruler to divide a single sheet of paper into three vertical columns. List any situation that provoked your emotions in the column to the left. In the middle column, describe your reaction. Then, in the column to the right, describe a more constructive response you could have taken:

SITUATION   YOUR REACTION   ALTERNATE RESPONSE

Keep this journal for at least two weeks, tracking your reactions to the situations that typically push your buttons and set off your attitude. Then take a good, long look at your entries. Compare your real-life reactions to these challenging situations with the alternate responses that could have helped you achieve more constructive outcomes.

Telling It Like It Is: Wielding Compassion

Avoiding control dramas and automatic reactions of rage helps you develop a capacity for a more genuine style of self-control I describe as "compassionate connecting." Compassionate connecting is the ability to express one's feelings, needs, and desires while remaining sensitive to the concerns of the other person. The goal of this method of relating is to use a more empathetic approach when relating to others. In this way, you can understand the other person's experience and reduce the possibility of conflict. You will be less reactive and more proactive toward your partner.

Many women believe that when they're screaming, making threatening gestures, and cursing their partners, they are powerful. In actuality, they are powerless and out of control. When all the tornado-like fury dies down, they are struck by a profound sense of their vulnerability and helplessness. The black women's favorite mantra is "I am strong, in control, and don't need nobody," so that underlying feeling of helplessness is particularly threatening. On the other hand, genuine power does not have to be aggressive or attacking. It can be more engaging and rewarding.

Anyone can learn to relate with compassion. All you need is a willingness to be patient, understanding, and open to win-win negotiations. I use the following comparison chart to illustrate the difference between "hostile but helpless" and "powerful and compassionate":

HOSTILE EXPRESSION	COMPASSIONATE EXPRESSION
Threatening body language	Body relaxed with open arms and legs
Name-calling	Use of person's real name or pet name
Cursing	Share real emotions
Interrupting	Allow the other person to finish
Yelling	Maintain even level of volume
Not listening to understand	Focus on other's words and meaning
Lack of eye contact	Look periodically into partner's eyes

Threatening or aggressive body language includes everything from hands on hips and folding your arms in front of your chest to standing too close, shaking a fist or finger, kicking a chair leg, punching a wall, or throwing something. When your arms and legs are relaxed and you face your partner fully, you indicate a willingness to communicate, you're "saying" that you are open to hearing whatever your partner has to say.

Name-calling invites your partner to shut you out, whereas use of his name or even an affectionate pet name invites him to take in whatever you have to say.

Cursing expresses blind rage, whereas sharing your true emotions in a noninflammatory manner gives him something real and substantive to consider.

Interrupting suggests that you are totally uninterested in your partner's thoughts and emotions, and it leaves you with little understanding of where your partner is coming from. If you allow him to communicate fully, without interruption, you gain better understanding of his position, and you show him that you are truly interested in knowing how he feels.

Yelling causes your partner to shut you out because he feels compelled to defend himself. Whenever anyone is in defensive mode, he is not open to the other person. He is too invested in protecting himself. So the screamer loses out, once again. No matter how loud she screams, she will never be heard.

Not listening to understand also leaves you ignorant of where your partner is coming from and ensures that the two of you will never understand each other's positions. Focused, or active, listening means you carry the intention of understanding. Not only will you better comprehend what your partner is trying to communicate, but he will also realize that you want to understand.

Refusing to meet your partner's eyes also suggests an unwillingness to hear him out. Maintaining periodic eye contact is another way to let him know that you are willing to share opinions and emotions and stay connected.

Chapman's Formula for Compassion

Moving from hostile conflict to expressing connection with compassion takes time and effort, but it's well worth it. Whenever sisters and brothers employ compassionate expression, they bypass blame and shame and start on the positive, constructive work that leads to true connection.

We've all been on the hostile end of a situation. And we've all picked the wrong time to bring up an important issue—in the middle of an argument about something else, for example, so that a small squabble blows up into a genuine crisis. Here's a simple strategy designed to keep you from heading down that dead end and move you instead toward a resolution brought about through compassionate expression. Whenever a situation threatens to get out of hand, consider the "3 C's":

1. Calm the Crisis

Once an argument starts, it can escalate to the point where we activate the negative coping mechanisms we are accustomed to using. Because neither of you can tolerate the other's negative coping mechanisms, the drama escalates as each person turns his or her focus away from trying to understand and toward trying to control each other.

The "time out/time in" technique used to discipline children can also be useful when adults are embroiled in an out-of-control confrontation. Whenever either member of a couple feels he or she is getting hot under the collar, I recommend asking for a time-out. The person who needs the time-out makes the request and also describes what he or she will do to cool down: take a walk, listen to music, do deep breathing, even watch the news on television. It doesn't matter what the activity is, as long as it is agreeable to both parties. The important point is that a time-out doesn't mean walking out the door and down to the corner bar. Everything about the time-out should be negotiated, including how long it will last. The "return time" must be honored because, again, we are not talking about storming off. Once both of you have agreed on the terms of the time-out, the environment will be much more conducive to reaching an agreement whenever you do return to the issue at hand. You will have moved from crisis and conflict to the possibility of agreement.

2. Correct the Course

The next important point is to make sure that you communicate whatever is on your mind in a way that doesn't make your partner defensive and land the two of you right back at square one, in crisis. I recommend a technique I call the Chapman Sugar Pill.

Hold back the real issue, which might be a bitter pill for your partner to swallow. Sugarcoat it by first acknowledging whatever is good and positive between you. People find it much easier to take in criticism whenever it follows positive statements. Then, when you do get down to the essence of whatever you want to tell him, make sure that you precede every statement with *I* instead of *you*. "*I* feel hurt whenever you keep me waiting past the time we were supposed to meet" instead of "*You* always keep me waiting past the time we were supposed to meet." Starting a statement with *you,* as in "You always make me wait for you," suggests you're about to launch a direct attack. That just puts him on the defensive.

If you've already made this complaint before, you can ask your partner which part of what you're trying to communicate is still unclear. Try to rephrase that information.

Finally, close your statement by telling him how much you value the relationship and why you want it to work.

3. Communicate and Connect

An open channel of communication keeps you functioning as a couple. Once you have managed the Sugar Pill technique, you want to keep the atmosphere friendly enough so that you can activate the technique whenever necessary. Keep the vibe comfortable by employing the following strategies for communicating and connecting:

- Check and reflect. To avoid starting a conflict, I ask people to check themselves before it's too late. This means turning the looking glass toward you and asking, "Is this really what I want to say?" If anyone were to keep score on the number of negative reactions that fly back and forth between couples during an argument, both parties would be shocked. So, before you snap and let an insult or dirty look jump out, give yourself time to reflect. You can also gain time by asking your partner to paraphrase whatever you've just said in order to make sure that you expressed yourself with accuracy and that he got your meaning.

- State what you're feeling directly. Don't talk about one issue when you are really concerned about another. For example, don't talk about how he smacks his lips when he eats when you're really upset that he broke your date last night at the last minute. Instead of merely expressing your displeasure, you need to reveal what is actually bothering you about his behavior. What is the real issue? Is it smacking his lips when he eats or the lack of consideration and care he showed by standing you up?

- Watch your vocal tone, volume, facial expression, and choice of words. Keep your vocal and physical mannerisms as calm and reasonable as possible.

- If you start feeling vulnerable, instead of going on a lengthy tangent to blow off steam, calm yourself with a few deep breaths and hold on to your chair until your body relaxes enough for you to express your feelings clearly in words.

- Be honest with yourself and your partner. This is the only way you will ever understand each other.

- If your partner says something nasty to you and you feel hurt, instead of becoming defensive and exchanging insults, try the "reversal" approach. For example, if he calls you a bitch, do not buy into that thought. Halt your natural defensive reaction in its tracks. Reverse the thought by reminding yourself that you are not what he's calling you. He's the one with the problem.

You wrote the
emotional script
that created your life.
Rewrite that script
for a healthier
attitude and a
better life.

Eight

Making Positive Connections

Free Your Mind for a Brighter Future

Once women are clear about what they want from life and love, they are in the best position possible to realize their desires. They can move from the pain of alienation to the fulfillment of connection.

Fuzzy thinking begets fuzzy results, but clarity negates the need to create the defense of bad attitudes. Clarity also keeps women from wasting time on situations and people that will give them only frustration and pain. As I've already told you, gaining clarity isn't easy. It takes time and relentless honesty, and you have to be willing to go through moments of discomfort to get where you need to be.

The first challenge for women struggling to form healthier

and more liberated attitudes is to learn how to work through emotional conflict. This experience can feel scary and overwhelming. Too many people run from emotional issues and conflicts because they automatically view conflict as negative, or they assume that conflict is a sign of trouble that cannot be overcome. Yet women who "hang in there" and work through their emotional conflicts are the ones most likely to be rewarded with durable and fulfilling relationships.

I can't promise that a changed attitude will guarantee you a life of bliss with Mr. Right, and I can't guarantee you'll even find him. But you still need to change your attitude because you have to live with yourself for the rest of your life. What I can promise is that a changed attitude leads to changed circumstances. If you want a different, more positive outcome, you must be willing to change the way you act and think. It's that simple and that complicated.

Gaining clarity involves entering a deeper part of your mind so you can reflect on your life's direction and how to change it. You must create the time and space to do this. This can be a big challenge. Women are usually so busy running around taking care of everyone else, or filling in downtime with all sorts of activities, that they don't create enough opportunities to be quiet and go within. That time for reflection is absolutely necessary if you want to explore your issues and make clear, informed decisions about what you want in life and whom you may want to share it with.

You also need to discover what keeps getting in your way. If you lack self-confidence, it is difficult to trust that you are capable of changing your life for the better. Change requires taking risks, entering the unknown, and trusting that you can take care of yourself. Self-trust is absolutely necessary to find courage to make the right strategic moves that will help you get the outcomes you desire. Again, it's important to realize that your behavior always results from your own decisions, whether you made them consciously or they seemed to have "just happened." Your attitude and behavior come from your own issues, not from the male shortage or a man's refusal to commit.

You and only you have full and complete control over the way you view the world and yourself and how you respond to any situation. *Responsibility* breaks down into *response* and *ability*, which emphasizes the word's meaning: You are able to choose your response.

Individuals who approach life with well-adjusted attitudes have accepted responsibility for their choices. That acceptance gives them self-confidence and the power to make healthier choices. They know that their behavior results from their own conscious and informed decision to be clear, honest, and rational.

When you hold yourself back in a reactive mode with a bad attitude, you allow your environment and others to control you. You lose your power because your emotions and actions are now tied to the behavior of others. According to Victor Frankel, the noted German philosopher, "There are three central values in life: the experiential—that which happens to us; the creative—that which we bring into our existence; and the attitudinal—our response in difficult or stressful situations."

I believe what matters most of these three values is the attitudinal, how we respond to life's challenges. Within this point of view, difficult situations are seen as opportunities to change the way we view our experience. These challenges help us make positive shifts in our beliefs and our behaviors. If our world is rocked, we are forced to make necessary adjustments in our thinking, attitude, and behavior, and we grow as human beings.

If you approach your man and the situation with the belief "There's nothing I can do about it," your behavior and your destiny are determined by that fundamental thinking and a sense that you are powerless. You are not viewing the situation clearly. The belief that you are helpless robs you of the ability to determine what your options are. This defeatist way of thinking leads many women to feel victimized and to create defensive attitudes.

Empowering yourself does not mean becoming masculine, rude, or abrasive. It means nothing more and nothing less than taking positive action to fulfill your goals and direct your own fate. Empowering yourself means that you trust yourself to make the right choices. Empowering yourself means you have the courage to stand up for yourself, especially with someone you love, and that you know you can take care of yourself no matter what.

The key element in owning your personal power is precisely this: being willing to express your point of view, to lay all your cards on the table, and to learn softer skills of negotiation, compromise, and submitting.

How much of your power have you claimed? Ask yourself the following questions whenever you are in a situation that requires you to take control of yourself and what happens to you:

1. What do I want?

2. What does the other person want?

3. Have I made my wishes clear?

4. Have I thought about what I need to do
   if the other person refuses to cooperate?

5. What is the least threatening way to convey
   my thinking and wants?

6. Am I willing to risk losing this relationship
   or not having my wishes fulfilled?

Rachel, the daughter of one of my friends, learned to take responsibility for her actions. Once she realized that being empowered means knowing that she is able to make the best choices, no matter what the situation, she was able to operate from a clear and positive attitude about her world.

Rachel had never been married. She was engaged for a year and a half, but called it off because her intended husband became overbearing and controlling. After a series of disappointing dates, Rachel decided to drop out of the social scene. She wound up dateless for about three and a half years, but she wasn't upset. She wanted to use this period alone to gain distance from her love patterns so she could view her social life with more objectivity and clarity.

She began reading self-help books, attending relationship workshops, seeking advice from an older woman in her sorority, and she even took a Bible class because she wanted to do something about her "moral judgment." Rachel also decided to go back to college to complete her bachelor's degree, so she wouldn't spend her life working as a secretary.

One day, her old car broke down. She brought it to a garage, where she noticed an attractive guy working on a car. She introduced herself and told him about her car troubles. Russell told her what he thought was wrong and said he would see her in a day or two to give her a recommendation and an estimate. When she returned to the garage, she flirted with Russell, but he maintained a purely professional demeanor. She began to feel irritated and wondered what was wrong. She paid for the estimate and told him she'd bring in the car to be repaired, even though she was more interested in returning so Russell could pick up on her vibes.

About a week later, Rachel returned with her car, not to get the repairs, but to ask Russell to change her oil. He still showed no interest. At that point, Rachel lost it a little and burst out, "Do you think I'm cute?" She knew her question was awkward, but she couldn't think of another way to break the ice. "Yes, but aren't you engaged?" he answered. "Isn't that a ring on your finger?" She had never taken off the diamond her fiancé had given her!

Once she explained that the engagement was over, matters warmed up immediately. They talked, and Rachel found Russell even more fascinating after he described his professional goals. He had real potential. Russell planned to own his own gas station someday soon; Rachel liked that he thought big. In the past, she'd always become involved with men because they were gorgeous, not because they had anything on the ball, let alone the confidence to set and pursue goals. Before she pulled away, they exchanged telephone numbers, and Russell called that night. They began going out.

They spent nearly four months talking about their intentions, goals, family backgrounds, and other parts of their personal histories. Eventually, they agreed to become "an item." About a year later, he proposed and they were married. Today, they're buying a house. Russell co-owns a gas station, and Rachel is finishing law school.

Russell believes he was able to do so well in his career and life because Rachel's got his back. Russell knew he needed a stable, secure, and healthy relationship in order to focus on his professional life. Likewise, Rachel believes that Russell supports her ambition to become the best woman she can be, and he helps her find the courage to pursue a degree in law and become the first person in her family to go beyond undergraduate school.

"Women should not settle," Rachel told me. "They should know that there will be some compromises, but they should always make sure that the man will want you for the long haul."

Rachel also credits the time she took off from the dating scene with allowing her to reassess her social life and become clear about what she really wanted and the changes she needed to make to fulfill those goals.

Think before you leap so you can first set your own goals. What do you want for your life right now?

Make a list right now of everything you want in your life—one list relating to family, another for work, another for friendships, and the last for men.

1.

2.

3.

4.

5.

6.

7.

8.

9.

10.

Now compare the list to the one you made on page 10 in chapter 1 concerning men. Are there any differences? If so, you're on your way to adjusting your attitude, as our expectations feed our attitude. The other lists are to help you see that your life and personal desires involve more than just romantic relationships.

Now that you've figured what you want in your life, you can better recognize someone with compatible aims and be open to a relationship with him. Rachel discovered early on in her talks with Russell that his goals were similar to hers, especially in his desire to find a stable and supportive relationship that would allow him to deal more effectively with the world.

Would you take a trip to a new and unknown destination without first consulting a map? Would a contractor erect a building without first securing a blueprint?

Unfortunately, many of us are either following the wrong maps or blueprints or flying blind. We don't even know when we're using maps other people wrote for us. Those old, tattered, worn-out maps and blueprints may have been handed down from childhood experiences or even borrowed from girlfriends who offer well-intentioned but misguided advice. We need to make out those life directions for ourselves.

Before she took her three-and-a-half-year sabbatical from men, Rachel was listening so intently to her friends' advice on life and love that she never stopped to consider who she was and what she really wanted. Once she took the time to figure all this out, she was able to tear up those borrowed directions and create her own plan.

If you find that you are flying without a map or using a map that doesn't apply to your own "territory," it's time to take a break and reconsider. Give yourself the space you need to gain clarity and draw up better directions.

The Sister Circle

We've talked about the importance of following your own life plan, instead of other women's, but other women can also be your greatest support system. Unfortunately, many sisters drop their friends faster than you can say "Taye Diggs" as soon as they land a man. Of course, as soon as the relationship is over, they want to pick up the friendships where they left off.

Even more disappointing, many sisters view other black women as competition. They're terrified of losing a man to a younger, prettier, richer female, yet they think nothing of romancing other women's husbands and boyfriends. In fact, some women will deliberately go after another woman's man simply to prove that she's better or that she can get away with it. Some women become involved with a married man without knowing it, but once they find out that the man is attached, they decide, "Too bad. We're just going to have to share him."

Yet if a sister finds out that her man is cheating on her with another woman, she can become far more enraged at the woman—who may be totally unaware of the man's double life—than at the man himself. These women will fight tooth and claw over a man while allowing him to escape unscathed.

When you view other women as the enemy, you are forfeiting your greatest potential support system. We've talked about learning and reinforcing compassion and the courage that can take. There's nothing like a circle of your sisters urging you on to help you be as patient, caring, and strong as possible.

I encourage you to assemble a group of female friends, a compassionate circle with whom you can develop new intimacy skills and receive support. I'm not talking about running partners, the girls you hang with in clubs. I'm talking about a support system of friends who are going to tell you more than "You go, girl." I'm talking about truth-telling sisters who will give you a shoulder to cry on and a reality check whenever you need it, no matter what you want to hear.

Without a full life, in which you relate closely to more than one person, you won't develop the mature intellectual, emotional, and spiritual self that you need to bring to a relationship with a man.

If a man doesn't seem to want you to have your sister circle, that's a good indication that he doesn't have your best interests in mind. He doesn't want anyone who cares about you to bust his game or influence your thinking.

During the eight years Monica had been with Ellis, she had gradually given up all her close friends. Now, whenever she and Ellis argued, she felt extremely vulnerable because she'd always think to herself, "Who would I have if Ellis and I ever broke up?" He had succeeded in his plan to isolate her and keep her all to himself, powerless and dependent on him.

Empowered Sisters and Insecure Brothers

One of the cruelest realities playing out today between black men and women is the penalty many sisters find they have to pay for having a strong sense of self and a belief in their own worthiness. This is particularly true of black women who have also distinguished themselves in their career.

Men make many assumptions about high-achieving women, including the assumption that they make much more money than the men earn. Brothers also assume that sisters in positions of authority, such as executives, attorneys, judges, physicians and psychotherapists, or owners of successful businesses, will be smarter, more insightful, more independent, and more comfortable with power. Men hate to think that they're going to become trapped in a situation in which they might feel overwhelmed and helpless.

One Sunday, I gave a presentation for a mostly female church group on the topic "How to Be a Healthy Woman in a Relationship with a Man." When I finished speaking, lots of people came up to me to get individual advice. Among them was a tall, stately, attractive woman of about thirty-five, with a walnut brown complexion and finely sculpted features. She was also well dressed and patient. She waited for most of the women to speak with me before she sat down next to me and said, "Quite frankly, I've given up on them." I realized that she meant black men.

"Why?" I asked. "Why would a woman with a presence such as yours give up on meeting men?"

"What I really meant to say is I'm tired of them."

"What are you so tired of?"

"Let me tell you what happens. I meet lots of men. I'm fairly social, and I belong to many associations, so I'm out all the time. Without a doubt, when I am out, I will meet a gentleman who wants to get to know me. We'll talk a bit and agree to get together another time. We'll exchange cards. Then, at some point, he asks me what I do for a living. I don't offer to tell them. In fact, I pray that they won't ask."

"Why?"

"Because whenever I tell them the truth, they clear away immediately, and they usually leave me just standing there."

"What could you do that could be so horrible that a man wouldn't want to relate to you?" I wondered aloud.

"I'm a judge. What I usually try to do is get around it by just saying that I work for the federal government. But they usually want to know exactly what my job is. After I tell them, they get this look on their faces, as if I just told them I'm a gravedigger. The next thing I know, they suddenly remember a phone call they have to make right away, and they're gone.

"I know you probably think this may have happened once or twice, but this story has repeated itself over and over, many times. There was the time when I met a guy I really liked; it was instant chemistry the moment we saw each other. We were at a party, so we didn't get much time to talk, but we agreed to catch up with each other by phone during the following week. We exchanged numbers. He called, and we did talk, and he said that he wanted to see me and didn't want to spend too much time on the phone. So we got together that afternoon for lunch. I made sure I wore one of my most attractive suits and did my hair a special way. I was really excited. We sat and talked and he finally brought up the subject of what he does for a living. He's a program analyst. He told me that he'd been out there for a long time, and he was tired of the rat race, and it was such a pleasure to meet a woman who seemed so self-assured. He went on praising my style and personality, and then he said, 'But, wait a minute. I don't even know what your job is.'

"At that point, I felt my stomach flip-flop and I felt I was close to panicking. I tried to be cool, because I didn't want him to see a side of me that would be alarming. I tried to figure out a way to get around his answer and be more indirect, so I said, 'I work with families.' And he said, 'Oh, that's nice. Are you a social worker?' I answered, 'Kind of, but not exactly.' 'Come on, tell me. I can handle it,' he said. 'It can't be that bad!' "

She then told me that she decided it was time for her to be more confident about telling men that she was a judge, so she forged ahead.

"I took a deep breath, and said, 'I'm a circuit court judge in the family division.' With that, I felt the connection between us break. I never really found out what happened. All I know is that he attacked me by referring to me as a woman in a man's job. He said he'd been out with my type before. I asked, 'What type are you referring to?' The next thing I knew, we were arguing. Needless to say, lunch ended early. I walked out of the restaurant, went into my office, closed the door, and just cried."

At that point, I told her, "It sounds like you're blaming yourself for the insecurities of these men. They've convinced you that you're the problem. Now you've become very defensive about your work, and you are losing confidence about your ability to attract and meet an emotionally healthy man."

"I've heard you many times over the air and in workshops recommend that women open up their options. I've had it with black men. I'm one step away from dating men of other ethnic groups and cultures."

"There's nothing like giving yourself more options."

She smiled. "I know. I don't know why I've waited so long."

Letting Go of Limits

Because many brothers are threatened by a sister's success and healthy self-esteem, empowered black women are in great need of increasing their options. Yet one dynamic that troubles me a great deal about sisters in general is a tendency to avoid any situation that's even a tiny bit off the beaten path. For example, many black women believe that the only appropriate places to meet a new man are in a club, at a party, a professional conference, or a music festival or concert. Meet a man on the street? On a bus? On the subway? Never! Sisters will rap with a man in a bar, but they'd refuse to speak to the same man if they were to meet him on the way to the store or on public transportation.

If I suggest that a client take a trip to, let's say, the Montreux Jazz Festival, an annual summer event in Switzerland, she'll mostly likely turn up her nose. Montreux is not immediately identifiable as an African-American event. It's not on the established circuit.

Which brings up another issue: dating outside your race, age bracket, or economic/professional class. Some sisters react negatively to these options, sometimes to the extreme that they can't even stand to see another sister who's made those choices for herself.

Part of the problem is that some sisters view men as either Jack the Ripper or a potential husband. Either extreme causes them to act inappropriately. Simply viewing a new man as an acquaintance who might possibly become a friend will lessen the pressure you put on yourself and open you up to the possibilities.

Sometimes, these friendships do grow into relationships, but that should never be the goal. Friendships with men are also wonderful when they're just that. In fact, a male friend can offer a neutral perspective on men's thinking and behavior, and he can also give you feedback on how you tend to present yourself as a woman. Since all good relationships start as friendships, having male friends teaches you better relationship skills. Even if a man stays your friend and never becomes your lover, he can satisfy your need to bask in those masculine vibes. Not to mention those occasions when you need a man as an escort.

I know one woman who's had a close male friend for over two decades. Their friendship has endured each of their divorces, parental illness and death, the death of a friend, raising children, career challenges, and even the purchase of new homes, when she advised him on decoration and he helped her move. The relationship has even smoothly negotiated that rite of passage in all male-female heterosexual friendships, the phase during which sexual attraction becomes an issue and must be negotiated.

Of course, starting out with a man as friends is a great way to really get to know each other, and if romance does develop, it will do so on the firm foundation of friendship.

I've stated earlier that empowered, successful sisters need to increase their options. In truth, *all* black women are in need of as many options as possible. They're more in need of increased options than any other group of women, since it's a pretty well-known fact that there simply aren't enough professional, high-income black men to go around. And, as I noted earlier, men who are lower down on the economic and social status ladder can reject a successful sister because they're just too intimidated. Sisters need to be more liberal-minded than everyone else because the statistics simply do not work in our favor.

Yet many black women refuse to accept this reality and to broaden their options. They complain about the "numbers game" or they fight amongst each other over the few black men who are left. They usually fail to think the situation through and come up with the logical answer to their dilemma.

One day, I was waiting in Washington, D.C.'s Union Station for a train to New York. It was delayed, and I fell into conversation with a woman who had captured the attention of everyone in the waiting room. She stood there calmly, diamonds sparkling from her fingers, wrists, neck, and ears; slim, tall, and elegant in a long, white taffeta formal gown. Something about her confident bearing led me to assume she was African.

"My God, that's an outstanding dress," I complimented her.

"Thank you," she answered. "I got it in Paris."

I must admit that I was surprised by her American accent. I was also surprised by her response to my next comment.

"I've been told that shopping in Paris is very expensive," I offered.

"Not at all. I go there all the time."

This was getting more interesting. "How often?"

"At least four or five times a year."

She told me that she stays in a flat that she rents from a friend, and that she knows all the inexpensive shops and restaurants.

"What group or organization do you go with?" I asked.

"I go alone. I always go alone."

Now I was really intrigued. The train arrived, and as we walked down to the platform, she mentioned her travels to Switzerland, England, Germany, Sweden, and other overseas locations. I assumed that she spoke many languages. She told me she only spoke English, but she'd never had difficulty relating and connecting to people during her travels. She explained that she preferred traveling alone because she finds her African-American sisters are not very adventurous. They tend to cramp her style.

"They don't do this, they won't do that," she said. "I just can't live in a box. Life is too good and exciting to do that to myself. I like options."

She told me that she also had no problem dating outside her race and had enjoyed relationships with a few white men in her time.

We got on the train and sat together. She was on her way to a party at the Republican National Convention in Philly.

"You're going to a formal without a date?" I marveled.

"Oh, I got a man, but I won't allow him to define my life. We do some things together and some alone, and this is one thing I chose to do without him. He brought me to the station and he'll pick me up tomorrow."

I thought that also was quite refreshing.

"Don't get me wrong," she said. "I don't sleep around, but I also feel comfortable enough with myself to enter a crowd of people I don't know and mingle and have fun. I refuse to be a boring stick-in-the-mud. I love this guy, but he's not my entire life. I'm forty-seven years old and I'm an architect. He's eleven years younger, and he works two jobs as a waiter. I met him in Jamaica."

We laughed when I suggested that, like Stella, she had got her groove back. She told me that he had relatives in D.C., and a few months after she'd returned to the States from Jamaica, he'd come up for a visit. About a year later, he immigrated to America and moved in with relatives in D.C., where she helped him find a job. Now he has his own place and she has hers.

"I don't really need a husband right now," she said. "I've already had one of those. But I love his company."

Then she looked me straight in the eye and made one of the most refreshing declarations I've ever heard come from a sister's mouth:

"I don't know why a woman my age would want an older man. What could he do for her? They're usually tired and bellyaching about something, and they're never sure what night their 'equipment' will work. I need a man with a strong back and a firm piece. I also need a man who's adventurous and fun. Can you tell me why I need an older man?"

"I think you've proven your point," I conceded. "And I believe that you're an authentic woman."

By now, the train was about to pull into Philadelphia, where she was getting off, so I thanked her for the interesting and enlightening conversation. As she descended from the train like the queen she is, I thought, "There goes a woman with no attitude."

So, my sisters, what about expanding your options? Must it be an African-American man? What about other men of color? East Indian men? Caribbean men? African men? Asian men? Latino men? And, yes, what about white men? What about blue-collar men? What about younger men? What about older men?

All women benefit from additional choices, but black women must provide themselves with even more choices to increase their social options. I'd like to share with you a piece of advice I give to all my clients and friends: create your own rainbow coalition.

Getting the Right Attitude

All the information, strategies, and tips you've received so far give you everything you need to start adjusting your attitude and taking control of your life. The following list puts it all together so that you can better absorb everything you've learned:

- Cultivate self-awareness. This is the first step toward becoming more aware of the emotions, behaviors, and attitudes that direct your life. You must confront yourself with honesty and forgive yourself for not being perfect. No one is perfect. Life is for learning. Just forge ahead with a clearheaded appraisal of your love and lifestyles so you can begin discovering whatever you need to change.

- Stop running from your feelings. Give yourself permission to experience them fully. It might seem as though once you got started, you would never stop crying, or that your rage could ignite the world. In fact, there is an end to your tears and a limit to your anger. Accepting and releasing bottled-up emotions will come as a huge relief. If you show the world an attitude of rage, your anger is masking pain, hopelessness, and sorrow. The anger is just a defense to keep you from becoming more vulnerable and to ease fears that you will take on even more hurt.

  As you know by now, the only way to lose that attitude is to identify the emotions and issues that lie beneath it. That means allowing yourself to express the anger so that you can release the tears.

- Accept responsibility. You and you alone have control over your life and your love style. If something goes wrong, don't rush to judge and blame others. Check yourself first. It could be that your behavior is being dictated by old, mistaken belief systems left over from a past experience that no longer applies. Even when a man is being out-and-out doggish, you still have to take responsibility for your choice to deal with him. Once you recognize that it's your choice, you are free to let him go.

- Control your emotions. There's a time for experiencing your emotions, and there's a time for snapping out of it and using a cool head to check out how your attitude may be promoting negative situations. Go through your pain, but don't wallow in it. Consider a new perspective. This pain can be most sharp when you realize that you have to let go of a man, but it's like pulling off a Band-Aid: the best way to do it is quickly.

One woman who called my radio show told me that she had been dating someone for six months and it looked as if this relationship could be permanent. But her ex-boyfriend was still calling and showing up at her door every now and then.

"How do you let go?" she wanted to know.

"What's keeping you holding on?" I asked back.

"I just don't want to hurt him."

"Are you going to be more hurt or less hurt when you lose the boyfriend you have now?"

She quickly realized that she didn't want to lose her current man. "I guess I have to tell my old boyfriend, the next time he calls, not to call anymore. And I guess when he comes to my door, I have to tell him not to trespass on my property."

I added that if he refused to heed her request, she shouldn't hesitate to do whatever she needed: call on male relatives or friends or even call the police and take legal action.

I know that, most of the time, you have to let go of the only man you have at the moment, but the woman who called my show had no guarantees either that her new relationship would work out. She was actually holding her old boyfriend in reserve, just in case.

Even if you don't have a safety net, if you know clearly what you need in a relationship and a man has proven he can't meet those needs, ask yourself this question: "Isn't it more painful to continue banging my head against the wall of a frustrating, unfulfilling relationship? Wouldn't it be less painful to let it go and give myself the chance of finding someone else who can love and care about me?"

- Change your thoughts. Your thoughts determine how you view a situation, which, in turn, determines how you behave. At the same time, negative patterns of behavior create their own belief systems. The point is this: your thoughts and behavior affect each other and shape the course of your love life. Every time you catch yourself thinking a negative thought about yourself and the helplessness of your situation, substitute for it a more realistic assessment of who you are and your real options.

- Embrace your mistakes. Learn to view so-called mistakes, heartbreaks, and crises in a new, more positive light. They are your lessons. Allow them to teach you and become major turning points that direct you toward a happier, healthier life filled with love. Instead of beating on yourself for every wrong turn, this constructive approach helps you challenge the self-doubts, fears, resentments, anger, and shame that block your path to change.

- Know that your dream man doesn't have to be perfect. Black women lose too much energy looking for superficial perfection in a man. If you are not perfect, why must he be? It frustrates me to hear women complain about silly nonsense in one breath, then tell me with the next that they can't take any more nights alone. Get rid of the following critiques: "He's too short." "He's got a stomach." "He's out of shape." "He's too light-skinned." "He wears frumpy suits." "His shoes are tired." "He doesn't make enough money." "He doesn't have a nice car." "His apartment is too messy." "His hair is all wrong." "He needs another degree." "What would my children look like with him?" "He's of a different race."

  What difference does any of this make? Superficial concerns yield superficial results. Black women need to spend their time on real possibilities, not on meaningless fantasies. The sister of today faces a new social paradigm—the reality that many black women are living in perpetual states of singleness. Don't resist opening your heart and mind to other options. You must do this if you are to have love in your life.

- Face your fears. Confronting your fears head-on may be one of your greatest challenges, but it brings you many

rewards. Your fears contain the key to your most important changes, because fear will rule your life and bring
you negative results. Only when you get past fear to
experience the confidence that comes from having challenged its hold over you will you be truly free of its
destructive effects. For example, many black women's
fear of rejection and being alone keeps them tied to relationships that make them miserable. Challenging that
fear by ending the relationship and allowing yourself to
be alone for a while will greatly empower you. You will
no longer make choices based on fear.

You can figure out what you're afraid of by keeping
close track of your mental chatter, the stories you make
up in your head. How extreme are they? What are the
typical scenarios? How you do feel as these stories play
out? What are your physical reactions? Typical signs of
fear are butterflies in the stomach, sweaty palms, chills,
tight muscles, and repetitive nervous tics.

Fear can also make you focus on one man and obsess
over him, like the character in the movie *Fatal Attraction.*
This person suddenly becomes your lifeline, and you're
fearful that without him you will be totally lost.

- Keep the faith. Never lose faith in yourself. Life isn't over
just because Mr. Right isn't with you at the moment.
Instead of focusing on the man you don't have yet, direct
your attention elsewhere. Get a life, even if it doesn't
include a man right now. During a group counseling session, when one woman was crying over the loss of her
boyfriend, another woman offered the following bit of

wisdom: "Men are like buses. If you miss one, wait, and another one will come along." That broke up the solemn mood. Everyone laughed, even the woman mourning her broken relationship. Sure enough, a few months later, she'd caught another bus.

- Be open to new experiences. Don't be like the women who restrict their opportunities to meet men. They will gladly arrange a date with a man they meet in a club, but they refuse to smile back at the stranger on the street or in the supermarket.

- Be responsive, not reactive. Being responsive means you have a clear and well-thought-out plan in mind, that you don't jump into situations. If you have an idea of what you need in a relationship, you will respond to how a relationship develops with awareness and honesty. That doesn't mean you try to control how events unfold, but you never lose sight of your goals and you're willing to think things out and take responsibility for your actions.

    One, realize that you are fully responsible for and able to determine the course of your life.

    Two, know that life may not always bring you exactly what you expect.

    Three, be thankful for what you have gained from each so-called bad relationship. Those gains include new lessons or new experiences. A good way to determine what benefits you have gained, even from troublesome relationships, is to make up a "gratitude list."

All you have to do is write down each and every emotional or tangible benefit that hindsight reveals to you as a positive outcome. These benefits could include everything from children to career advice to better information on how to tell when a man is cheating.

Do this here:

GRATITUDE LIST

1.

2.

3.

4.

5.

Add as many additional benefits as possible. Remember: No matter how painful, relationships are the practice grounds where we work out whatever lessons we entered this life to learn.

Read your gratitude list over whenever you experience self-punishing regrets, self-doubts, fear, or whenever life and love appear to be hopeless. The basic point is that it's all good.

Life is challenging and, for some of us, quite difficult. But life can work for you rather than against you, once you understand that attitude is everything because *attitude is the only part of your life over which you have absolute control.*

Loving the Right Man

Life is amazing; you never know where or how you're going to meet someone. One evening, I met a couple at an art reception. Actually, I met the woman first, when she approached me, asking, "Do you remember me?"

She reminded me that ten years ago I had conducted a discussion for her women's group in Silver Spring, Maryland. This group meeting was unusual in that they had opened it up to men for a discussion on the usual topic: "How to find love and make it work."

The sisters in the group were from age thirty-five and up, and most of them had never been married, but they had decided to take matters into their own hands. Every other month, they invited single men to a relationship discussion, followed by coffee and tea. Of course, the hidden agenda was the hope that some women would invite single men whom other women could meet. The talk went well, and I didn't think much about the group again.

Now, here was one of those women telling me that she wanted to "introduce you to my husband."

"How interesting!" I said with a smile.

"We met at that singles event where you spoke," she informed me. Her husband came over to join us.

"We really appreciated many of the issues you raised about relationships and becoming more effective at loving," he said. "We went on discussing those issues for many months. We've now been married for eight years."

"And we've been *happily* married for all of those eight years!" his wife added in a whisper. I guess she still couldn't trust her good fortune and didn't want to risk jinxing it with a bold declaration!

If you think that women's group had a plan, let me tell you about a friend of mine. She actually mailed out her résumé to all her friends, along with an explanatory cover letter: "You don't need to be reminded of what I've done professionally. But I'm including my résumé just to let you know that I'm seeking a man who would appreciate someone like me." The letter went on to describe in precise detail just what kind of man she was looking for. She covered such characteristics as his morality, social experience, and religious beliefs. She even indicated that she preferred a nonsmoker, but if the man was right in other ways, she wrote, she could work with it. She wanted a worldly, fairly sophisticated, sociable, educated man, but she concluded by mentioning that race was of little concern.

Friends did come up with candidates; some of them were friends, others business associates. After a couple of years of serious dating—and the operative word here is *serious*—she met her husband. They've been happily married for sixteen years.

You don't have to paper your hometown with your résumé. Your man could be right under your nose. One happy couple I know met on the subway. They both took the same train every morning at the same time. Robert noticed Rita's face and thought she was beautiful. She was struck by his well-tailored, periwinkle blue shirt. For weeks, they stood in the same car, together but apart.

One day, Robert smiled at Rita, and she noticed how sweet that smile was. Soon they began chatting together on their daily commute. After a few months, Robert asked Rita to lunch. That lunch led to steady dating and, eventually, to a happy marriage. But if Rita had refused to return Robert's smile or to give him her telephone number, they might still be single and far less happy. If Rita hadn't been open to meeting someone on the subway, she would have lost out.

Women often find Mr. Right only after they've taken enough time to figure out why they have been getting involved with a series of Mr. Wrongs. A friend of mine named Camille had had several unhappy relationships. Every time she met a man, she believed he was the one, simply because she was nice and a professional and, therefore, was ready for a relationship. However, it never seemed to work out. One day, she realized that she needed time off from the dating market. In fact, she wound up forming a plan to be with herself alone until she could remove any self-imposed pressure and learn to enjoy her own company.

This was not an impetuous decision made out of disappointment, bitterness, cynicism, or anger. It was a conscious, self-fulfilling step toward a better life. Camille was tired of the players. "I needed to clean house," she said. "If I was being mistreated, I must have been a willing participant. That realization seemed to soften and change my attitude."

She began traveling, joined a tennis club, started a memoir about a famous relative, and in general, got herself a life. One day a friend invited her to a dinner party. She didn't want to go, but her friend insisted. She wound up spending time with a nice man named John. They went out on one date, and they really liked each other. There was a lot of excitement and energy. Camille couldn't believe this had happened without any pressure or urgency. They agreed to see each other again, but Camille didn't hear from him.

"What was different this time," Camille says, "was that I didn't panic. Before, I would have needed to know why he didn't call, why he didn't like me, and if I would ever hear from him."

This time, Camille had just come off four years of her time-out, and the strength and confidence she'd gained ensured that she didn't panic.

"Thank God, I was in a good place with myself," she told me. "I no longer was afraid to be alone. I knew I could survive, with or without him."

Seven months later, as she was at home writing on her computer, the phone rang. It was John.

"I was just sitting here, thinking about you," he said.

"Oh, really?" Camille replied.

John then told her that his life had been confusing, with many changes, and he just couldn't handle anything more. But life had settled down and he was ready to see her, if she was still available. Camille didn't have an attitude holding her back, so she wasn't emotionally invested in his "rejection." She was open to seeing John.

They dated for three months and spent a lot of time together. Camille had also departed from her past pattern of leaping right into bed with a new man, and she decided not to be sexual. She told John that she was not interested in sleeping with him right away, and that if he was looking for that, she understood. But John said he felt the same way. Once that was squared away, they began to develop a genuine relationship. After the three months, they began sleeping together and decided their relationship would be exclusive.

It's been two years now, and they're talking about buying a house together. They're also making plans for a small wedding somewhere down the road.

<u>What Brothers Need to Do for Love</u>

><(Accept that commitment brings its own rewards, such as emotional and financial stability, intimacy, security, a deep sense of sharing, and someone to count on.

><(Work with all your heart and soul to be honest, faithful, and loyal.

><(Don't expect more from your woman than she is able to give.

><(Develop a centered self to avoid being self-centered.

><(Talk to your woman tenderly about the issues closest to your heart.

><(Don't make promises you can't keep and keep the promises you do make.

><(Respond to your woman's desires without her always having to ask.

><(Try to listen actively and empathetically instead of telling your woman what to do.

><(Be willing to own your mistakes and to apologize for them.

><(Learn to explain instead of blame.

><(Allow for each other's social space. Don't possess.

><(Don't try to control your woman's personality. Accept her as she is.

><(Give your woman lots of affection, support, and encouragement.

Remember to ask for guidance when any item
on the above list seems too difficult to fulfill.

<u>What Sisters Need to Do for Love</u>

▶◀ Work at being honest and loving toward your man.

▶◀ Try to be attentive to your man's needs and wants without resentment.

▶◀ Offer your man compliments when it's appropriate.

▶◀ Work with all your heart and soul to be faithful to your man.

▶◀ Be available to your man's emotional needs without smothering him.

▶◀ Don't attack. Listen with an active ear before sharing your opinion.

▶◀ Keep your word.

▶◀ Accept that men need physical and emotional space from time to time, as society hasn't encouraged men to learn how to express their emotions.

▶◀ Be willing to own your mistakes and to apologize for them.

▶◀ Invite your man to share his feelings and issues about the relationship.

▶◀ Earn your man's trust by being consistently open and honest with your feelings.

▶◀ Don't let your attitudes dictate your moods.

▶◀ Accept your man as he is.

▶◀ Give your man lots of affection, support, and encouragement, especially during difficult times.

Remember to ask for guidance and understanding whenever an item on the above list seems too challenging to fulfill.

You are what you
think, and what you
think determines
what you do.

Epilogue

Finding and Keeping Love

Something has happened to all Americans over the past four generations or so. Instead of showing each other compassion, consideration, patience, and other loving behaviors, our world has become full of road and air rage, domestic violence, divorce, kids shooting kids, and men and women jockeying for power. It especially confuses me when I think of black people's frustrations in love, because we're often thought of as people with a natural passion for one another.

Yet, the practice of loving action sometimes seems missing altogether from our collective life. Did we lose it by adapting to the greater society's definition of love? Did we assimilate too much? Are we still suffering from the victimization of slavery and that institution's total disregard for the sanctity of families?

Whatever the reasons, at the dawn of this new millennium, black people, like everyone else, are more afraid than ever of commitment, closeness, and marriage, despite so many people's loud insistence that they're searching everywhere for love. Sadly, these people don't understand that you can't find love if you don't even understand what it is.

I understand the anger and pain, but the black community has been paying the price for a war that seems to have no resolution. *It must stop!* Black women must realize that good men are out there. Black men need to realize all black women have ever wanted was to love them and be loved, and that the tensions between the sexes are not about the women's lack of love for the men but an expression of their painful experiences. It's difficult to love someone who won't let you into his heart.

Falling in love is the easy part. Having a passionate affair is fun. The challenge is making love last and grow into something solid and strong. We fail to realize that love, like all intense emotions, continually changes, dissolves, and transforms. Love is not solid and fixed; it is fluid and mutable. When it is successful, love is intimate and responsive to the loved person. We all say we want love, and at times we may even move toward it, staying longer than we expected or for a briefer time than we desired. There are lessons to be drawn from all experience—good, bad, and indifferent. Challenging and difficult experiences teach about love, increase our self-awareness, and show us the ways to make love last.

We must honor and cherish the love that forms the core of a lasting relationship. Sensitivity to the needs of the partner is crucial, trying to avoid inflicting pain is essential, as are encouraging your partner to be whole and giving him respect as a human being. Love dies when too little attention is paid to cultivating the above elements because you're overly focused on what's missing and what's wrong with the relationship, and you spend too much time battling and hurting each other. You have to listen to your partner and accept that the challenges of your relationship are opportunities for your own growth. And you have to love each other "as is." Attempts to make him over only damage the quality of the relationship. People only change when they decide to.

I'm not suggesting, though, that, if you are in an abusive relationship and careful evaluation confirms that this man will never meet your needs, you should stick with it, at all costs. You have to be clear about what is not good for you, and you should always be in control and self-protective. Here's a good rule of thumb: if it hurts too much, it's probably not good for you.

Real love is creatively bonding with the other, and receiving, accepting, and affirming that love. Black men and women are in dire need of this healing experience, today more than ever before. If you find that you do not feel loved as much as you wish, you may be suffering even more from your own inability to make love happen within yourself and to give love to another. Are you prepared to give love in this deep and committed way?

Brothers and sisters, if loving each other is your goal, then we must all begin to change the messages we've been giving each other about love. We cannot survive in America without this basic alteration in our collective mind-set. If we could accept that as men and women we are different but complementary, yet so similar in our deepest emotional needs, we would live together in greater peace and harmony.

My wish is for us to begin coming together in small neighborhood groups, all across this country, to define, design, and commit to ways that will make us more sensitive, respectful, and loving of each other. If we can practice these new understandings, we won't judge; we will love with compassion. Only then will we get on with the business of finding love and making it last.

Love stays when you don't want to go away from it. Love stays when it becomes safe, comfortable, and responsible. I believe love stays when it has no other place to go.

We are a loving culture. We know that loving is better than not loving, and we also know that trusting is better than not trusting. We must stop rehashing never-ending conflicts that have been drawn out over too many generations. We must pick up the banner of love before it's too late. If we don't, the tensions and hurts will build until many of us are wounded beyond healing.

If we could join each other as a united force to find love and become more loving, we could stop our war and get on with supporting and loving each other, for better or for worse.

Lecture Information

Seven Attitude Adjustments for Finding a Loving Man was inspired by the many women and men throughout the country who have experienced inner discoveries, transformations, and made new choices about their love lives. Some of these individuals have attended Audrey B. Chapman's relationship seminar lectures.

At a time in this country when African-Americans need solutions for their personal problems, Chapman's seminar lectures provide advice on reducing stress points within intimate relationships, while creating a safe and supportive environment in which to explore these issues.

Among the many topics that may be presented are

- getting love right
- resolving conflicts
- managing anger with more compassionate expressions
- handling disappointments without backlashes
- dealing with fears and stressful situations without controlling your partner

To schedule an event contact

A. B. Chapman Associates, Inc.
1800 Diagonal Rd., Suite 600
Alexandria, VA 22314
(703) 518-4186

or

Barbara Vance Speakers Unlimited, Inc.
8201 Sixteenth Street, Suite 708
Silver Spring, MD 20910
(301) 608-3522
E-mail: suivance@aol.com

To organize compassionate circles in your community, visit our web site on organizing small groups of fifty to one hundred women seeking skills that will establish greater intimacy with men through compassionate expressions. To visit Chapman's Web site:

http://www.Audreychapman.com

Index

About the Author

AUDREY B. CHAPMAN is a nationally known authority on male-female relationships. In nearly twenty years, through her work as a therapist in private practice, she has seen several thousand individuals. She is the host of a weekly radio talk show, *The Audrey Chapman Show,* on WHUR-FM, and frequent lecturer and workshop facilitator. She has provided alternative solutions for the myriad problems and changes men and women face in their various social roles.

Chapman has conducted seminars and training sessions at Columbia University; Yale University; U.S. Air Force, Army, and Navy; Congressional Black Caucus; Library of Congress; U.S. Federal Reserve Board; National Council for Negro Women; National Association of Black M.B.A.s, Inc.; Smithsonian Institution; Delta Sigma Theta Sorority; Hampton University; and many other national institutions and corporations.

Ms. Chapman has published many articles and received numerous awards for her work and leadership in mental health. She is the author of *Mansharing: Dilemma or Choice?* and *Getting Good Loving: How Black Men and Women Can Make Love Work.* She has been interviewed by the *Wall Street Journal,* the *New York Times,* the *Washington Post, U.S. News Today, Essence, Ebony, New Black Women, Redbook,* and many others. She has appeared on such nationally televised shows as *Donahue, Oprah, Sally Jessy Raphael, 20/20, Maury Povich, Tony Brown's Journal,* and B.E.T.'s *Tavis Smiley Show* and *Heart and Soul Show.*

Ms. Chapman is a member of the National Board of Certified Counselors, Inc., and the president of A. B. Chapman Associates, Inc.